AI in Agriculture: Farming the Future

GoodMan, Volume 1

Patrick Mukosha

Published by Patrick Mukosha, 2025.

AI in Agriculture: Farming the Future

Precision Agriculture, Crop Prediction, Autonomous Tractors, and Smart Irrigation Systems.

Copyright Notice

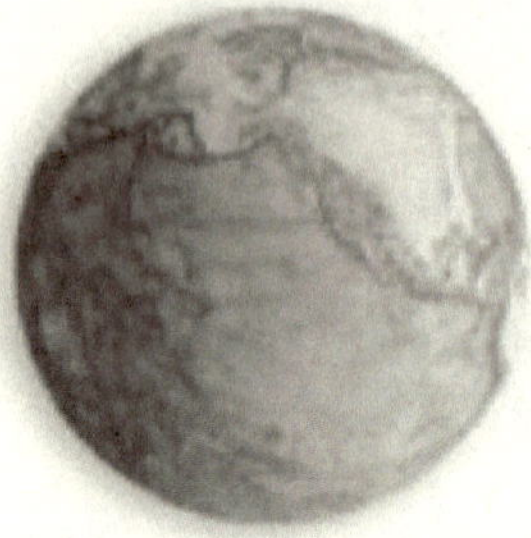

First published: August, 2025

Publisher: Patrick Mukosha PhD

Trademarks

Warning and Disclaimer

Author: Patrick Mukosha PhD

Abstract

Agriculture, the oldest and most important industry in the world, is going through a significant upheaval in a time when technology is changing every facet of human existence. The book ***AI in Agriculture: Farming the Future*** examines how AI is changing how we manage resources, produce food, and ensure the agricultural future of the world.

AI is revolutionizing farming from the ground up, from autonomous tractors and drones that work tirelessly efficiently to crop prediction models that anticipate yields with previously unheard-of accuracy to precision agriculture that identifies the precise requirements of every plant. *This book offers a thorough examination of state-of-the-art technologies including agri-neural interfaces, AI-driven climate resilience plans, and smart irrigation systems—where people and technology collaborate harmoniously to maximize food production.*

The book explores the economic, environmental, and social effects of AI-powered farming in addition to the technology, drawing on the most recent worldwide research, real-world case studies, and future-focused scenarios. In addition to addressing the issues of data ethics, farmer training, and fair access to technology, it tackles the promise of increased yields, decreased waste, and sustainable resource usage.

AI in Agriculture: Farming the Future presents a convincing picture of how humanity can use AI to feed a growing population, fight climate change, and develop a more intelligent, environmentally friendly, and resilient agricultural system, regardless of whether you are a policymaker, agricultural entrepreneur, tech innovator, or just an interested reader.

"The future of farming is not just in the fields—it's in the Algorithms." - Patrick Mukosha

Chapter 1: Overview – The Fourth Industrial Revolution (4.0)

Overview

The 21st century presents a conundrum for humanity. Food insecurity still threatens billions of people, despite the fact that technical breakthroughs have never been more significant. Food security is threatened by population growth, climate change, and the depletion of arable land. The answer? Ancient agricultural knowledge and artificial intelligence come together in this blend of tradition and change.

"AI in Agriculture: Farming the Future" examines how artificial intelligence is changing the agriculture industry. We are seeing an unprecedented change, from self-driving tractors that plough with mathematical precision to sophisticated sensors that track the health of the soil in real-time. This is a revolution in farming, planning, and thinking, not just automation.

Seeds and soil are no longer the only components of agriculture. These days, it's a data and decision domain. With the use of precision tools, prescriptive analytics, and predictive insights, AI enables farmers to maximize output by optimizing all inputs, including labour, water, and fertilizer.

This book is intended for farmers, technologists, legislators, and creative thinkers who recognize that food isn't only grown but engineered for the future.

1.1. A Synopsis of Agricultural Revolutions from Plough to Processor

Human civilization has traditionally been based on agriculture. Every significant advancement in agricultural evolution has changed society, from the Neolithic revolution, when people switched from hunting to farming, to the Industrial Age's mechanization.

Three significant agricultural revolutions have already occurred in the world:

1. The domestication of plants and animals during the First Agricultural Revolution (10,000 BCE).

2. Improvements in crop rotation, selective breeding, and mechanization throughout the Second Agricultural Revolution (17th–19th centuries).

3. Food production was significantly increased during the Green Revolution (1940s–1960s) by high-yield crops, chemical fertilizers, and irrigation technology.

We are now on the cusp of the *Fourth Agricultural Revolution, or Agriculture 4.0, which is fuelled by the combination of data science, robotics, AI, machine learning, and remote sensing.*

1.2. Agriculture 4.0: Definition

The term *"Agriculture 4.0"* describes *the Fourth Agricultural Revolution, a revolutionary period in which automation, data intelligence, and digital technology are driving farming.* This new phase incorporates artificial intelligence (AI), the Internet of Things (IoT), big data analytics, robotics, and smart sensors into every step of the agricultural value chain, building on the mechanization of Agriculture 1.0, the green revolution of Agriculture 2.0, and the early automation and biotechnology of Agriculture 3.0.

Agriculture 4.0 has more of an *emphasis on accuracy, sustainability, and connection* than earlier revolutions, which were largely concerned with boosting productivity through physical and chemical means. Farmers are becoming data-driven decision-makers who use autonomous machinery, real-time monitoring systems, and predictive models to maximize outputs while reducing environmental effect. They are no longer merely land cultivators.

Among the main features of Agriculture 4.0 are:

- Hyper-precision farming, which uses AI and IoT to customize pesticides, fertilizer, and water for specific plants or zones.
- Autonomous operations using robotic harvesters, drones, and driverless tractors.
- Predictive analytics for climate adaptation, pest identification, and crop yield forecasts.
- Sustainable resource usage, guaranteeing effective management of energy, water, and soil.
- Blockchain and AI-powered integrated supply chains for traceability and transparency.

Agriculture 4.0 is essentially a transition from conventional farming methods to automated, intelligent, and linked agricultural ecosystems that can feed the world's expanding population while protecting its resources.

1.3. Why AI in Agriculture Right Now?

The use of AI in farming has increased due to a number of worldwide trends:

- **Climate Change:** Crop productivity is at risk from droughts, irregular rainfall, and extreme weather events.
- **Population Growth**: By 2050, there will be more than 9.7 billion people on the planet, necessitating a 70% increase in food production.
- **Lack of Workers:** In many nations, there is a scarcity of agricultural workers as a result of rural-to-urban migration and aging farmer populations.
- **Resource Limitations**: Efficiency is now essential due to the scarcity of land and water.

By improving decision-making, maximizing input utilization, and accurately predicting outcomes, artificial intelligence provides solutions to these difficult problems that humans cannot match on their own.

1.4. AI in Practice: Real-World Applications

1.4.1. Case Study 1: Blue River Technology (USA)

Blue River Technology, which was purchased by John Deere, created the "See & Spray" technology, which employs deep learning and computer vision to precisely identify and eradicate weeds. Herbicide use has decreased by up to 90% as a result, lowering expenses and their negative effects on the environment.

1.4.2. Case Study 2: The Plantix App by PEAT (India/Germany)

The **Plantix App** analyses smartphone photographs to identify nutrient deficits, pest infestations, and plant illnesses using AI-powered image recognition. The app, which is widely used in India, gives smallholder farmers access to professional diagnosis and treatment guidance.

1.4.3. Case Study 3: Israel's Prospera

In greenhouse settings, **Prospera** employs artificial intelligence (AI) and computer vision to monitor plant health, identify irregularities, and maximize fertilizer and irrigation. The technology has the ability to forecast illnesses before their symptoms become apparent.

1.4.4. AI-Driven Change in Smallholder Agriculture

Although industrial farms are typically thought of as having high-tech agriculture, *AI is also finding its way into smallholder farms, particularly in South Asia and Africa.* Through SMS or smartphone apps, mobile-based AI systems like as CropIn, Sencrop, and Hello Tractor provide market prices, predictive weather alerts, and even tractor rental services. At the local level, this democratization of AI is increasing food security and changing livelihoods.

1.4.4.1. **Diagram: Benefits of Predictive Food Systems**

Benefit	**Description**
Food Security	Enhances planning and distribution of food where and when its needed most
Climate Adaptation	Uses simulation-based planning to assist farmers in adapting to erratic weather conditions.
Supply Chain Stability	Reduces post-harvest loss by coordinating production and logistics.
Risk Mitigation	Prevents market crashes, pests, and droughts before they happen
Resource Efficiency	Minimizes input waste by just using water and fertilizer when needed.

Figure 1: Benefits of Predictive Food Systems

1.5. Future Directions: What AI in Agriculture Will Do Next

1.5.1. As AI Advances, the Opportunities Increase By an Order of Magnitude

Artificial intelligence (AI) is driving the fourth agricultural revolution, which is a current change rather than a far-off promise. But the issue still stands: what comes next? *Agriculture will become more intelligent, robust, and predictive in the future as AI systems learn, self-optimize, and interact with other cutting-edge technologies like blockchain, quantum computing, nanotechnology, and synthetic biology.* One of the most intriguing developments is in Predictive Food Systems, where AI plans, anticipates, and anticipates agricultural results in addition to managing farming.

1.5.2. Predictive Food Systems: A Data-Driven for Global Agriculture

Vision and Definition

Big data, machine learning, real-time sensors, and sophisticated analytics are all used by predictive food systems to forecast all facets of the food lifecycle, including crop selection, production, pest outbreaks, supply chain interruptions, and consumer demand trends. Changing agriculture from a reactive to a proactive science is the aim.

How It Operates

Multiple data layers are integrated to operate predictive food systems:

- Satellite imaging provides meteorological information, plant health, and soil moisture.
- Internet of Things devices for field measurements in real time (e.g., crop stress, water flow, fertilizer levels).
- Genomic and historical data for crop behaviour modelling.

- Information from the market and logistics to forecast food demand and maximize distribution.

In order to provide actionable insights weeks, months, or even seasons ahead of time, these data points are fed into AI models that are constantly learning and developing.

1.5.3. Case Study: AgriStack in India and the Development of Predictive Models

In order to generate digital crop models, the **Agristack Project in India** seeks to consolidate agricultural data from millions of farms and integrate it with AI platforms. In order to forecast which crops farmers should plant based on localized weather models, market demand, soil health, and historical yield performance, Microsoft teamed up with the Indian government. Pilot projects demonstrated a 12% decrease in water consumption and a 17% increase in yield, demonstrating the effectiveness of predictive decision-making.

1.5.4. Case Study: IBM Watson in Kenya's Coffee Belt

In the Kenyan highlands, farmers were able to apply focused interventions only when necessary by using **IBM's AI Watson** platform to track the health of coffee crops and forecast pest outbreaks up to four weeks in advance. This maintained yield levels while reducing chemical usage by 30%.

Future Potential

Predictive food systems should be able to:

- Identify hotspots for global food insecurity before crises arise, as AI systems develop.
- Decades in advance, model how local crop performance will be impacted by climate change.
- To reduce risk and increase resilience, model different planting techniques.
- Forecast trends in consumer preferences using dietary changes, e-commerce data, and social media.

1.6. Integration with Other Technologies

- Blockchain will give predictive models safe provenance trails so they may verify their hypotheses with actual results.
- Even in places with inadequate internet connectivity, Edge AI will provide real-time predictions at the farm level.
- By managing intricate simulations involving several variables that conventional computers find difficult to handle, quantum computing has the potential to dramatically improve the accuracy of food system models.

1.7. Considerations for Policy and Ethical Aspects

There is great promise for improved productivity, sustainability, and food security through the application of artificial intelligence (AI) in agriculture. But in order to guarantee justice, inclusion, and responsible deployment, this technological revolution also brings up difficult ethical and policy issues that need to be resolved. AI-driven agriculture runs the potential of worsening inequality, damaging the environment, or eroding traditional farming knowledge in the absence of established guidelines.

1.7.1. Ownership and Privacy of Data

- **Problem:** AI systems for agriculture mostly depend on vast amounts of environmental and farm data.
- **Risk:** If companies gather, keep, and profit from farmers' data without their permission, farmers may no longer have control over it.
- **Policy Approach:** Provide clear data ownership rights, along with mechanisms for informed consent, anonymisation, and equitable data-sharing agreements.

1.7.2. Bias and Fairness in AI Models

- **Problem:** If algorithms are trained on biased datasets, they may inadvertently favour certain regions, crop types, or large-scale farms.
- **Policy Approach:** Encourage transparent and explainable AI models, require bias testing, and make sure datasets represent diverse agricultural contexts.

1.7.3. Intellectual Property (IP) and Technology Access

- **Problem:** Proprietary AI tools and patents may restrict access to advanced farming technologies for smaller or resource-poor farmers.
- **Risk:** Creates a digital divide whereby only large agribusinesses can afford AI-driven solutions.
- **Policy Approach:** Promote public-private collaborations, open-source AI solutions, and subsidized access to crucial agricultural AI tools.

1.7.4. **Sustainability and the Environment Issues**

- **Problem:** Although AI can maximize the utilization of resources, if economic motives take precedence, it may also promote overproduction, mono-cropping, and ecologically detrimental practices.
- **Policy Approach:** Integrate environmental effect evaluations into AI tool approvals and align AI deployment with sustainable agriculture policies.

1.7.5. **Using Automation Ethically**

- **Problem:** Employment in rural areas may be impacted by the replacement of manual work by autonomous machines and robots.
- **Risk:** Upheaval of society and loss of means of subsistence in agriculturally reliant communities.
- **Policy Approach:** To generate new job opportunities, implement retraining programs, workforce transition programs, and rural development policies.

1.7.6. **Cross-Border Data Flows And Global Governance**

- **Problem**: Agricultural AI systems frequently handle data from several nations, which presents concerns about compliance and sovereignty.

- **Policy Approach:** Create global agreements for the exchange of agricultural data while making sure that local laws and moral standards are followed.

1.7.7. **Integration with Traditional Knowledge**

- **Problem:** The use of AI could eclipse the centuries-old farming practices that have supported communities.

- **Policy Approach**: Promote hybrid models that honour cultural heritage by fusing traditional ecological methods with AI discoveries.

1.7.8. **Key Takeaway:** Strong regulations and moral protections must be incorporated into AI's development, application, and governance for it to have a transformational and fair impact on agriculture. This guarantees that technology developments benefit all parties involved, from small-scale farmers to multinational agribusinesses, without sacrificing social justice or environmental sustainability.

Important questions come up as national food strategies incorporate predictive food systems:

- *Who owns the models and data?*
- *How is algorithmic bias prevented for smallholder farmers?*
- *Is it possible for governments to resist the need to use food geopolitics prediction systems as weapons?*

1.8. Looking Ahead: A Future Driven by Prescience

Agriculture's future era will be characterized by prescience—the capacity to foresee and influence events before obstacles or opportunities arise—rather than just response. Agriculture will transition from a reactive system to one that is proactively directed by foresight thanks to AI's increasing predictive power.

1.8.1. **From Prediction to Knowledge**

Farmers used to make plans based on experience and seasonal tendencies. Climate simulations, satellite imagery, genomic data, and market analytics are being combined by modern AI algorithms to predict crop performance, insect outbreaks, and resource requirements weeks or even months in advance.

Because of this change, farmers can take action before dangers arise, turning uncertainty into opportunity.

1.8.2. **Digital Farm Twins' Ascent**

Virtual farm duplicates, or digital twins, will become commonplace tools. Before it affects crops, these simulations will:

- Forecast soil nutrient depletion.
- Suggest targeted actions, including modifying watering schedules or micro-dosing nutrients.
- To optimize planting methods against possible weather or market fluctuations, model "what-if" scenarios.

1.8.3. **Food Supply Stability and Market Expectations**

Predictive analytics from AI will be used in global food systems in addition to farms:

- Farmers will pre-align production with market demand, lowering waste and price volatility.

- Governments and agribusinesses will anticipate food shortages and take proactive steps.
- This insight could stabilize food prices worldwide and significantly lower the probability of famine.

1.8.4. **Forward-Looking Sustainability**

Additionally, predictive AI will support environmental objectives:

- Recognizing the ideal crop rotation schedules for soil health.
- Predicting the loss of biodiversity and offering conservation measures before serious harm is done.
- Organizing resource utilization to reduce environmental effect while maintaining efficiency.

1.8.5. **Human-AI Synergy in Decision-Making**

Future agricultural leaders will collaborate with AI to develop strategies rather than only relying on it to assist in decision-making. *AI will reveal opportunities*; people will assess the long-term socioeconomic, ethical, and cultural ramifications to make sure technology is consistent with human values.

1.8.6. **Important Takeaway:**

Prescience—foreseeing and influencing events instead of responding to them—will define farming's future. AI will increasingly respond to farmers' questions about "*what will happen next, and how can I prepare today?*" rather than merely "*what should I do now?*"

Redefining agriculture as a proactive, predictive, and resilient system that can sustainably feed the world will come from this move from reaction to foresight.

1.9. Independent, Self-Educating Farms

Automation's Next Step

Drones and self-driving tractors are only the beginning. Future farms will be entirely self-learning ecosystems run by AI bots that, without direct human intervention, plan logistics, harvesting, irrigation, sowing, and even economic decisions.

Important Attributes:

- **Self-Optimizing Equipment**: Drones and robots modify their activities in response to weather, crop response, and topography as they continuously learn from real-time data.
- **Integrated Decision Engines**: A central AI platform controls every aspect of farming, including when to plant, when to use pesticides, when to harvest, and even when to sell.
- **Robotic Swarms:** Tiny, nimble machines that cooperate to do activities like weeding, fertilizer micro-spraying, and monitoring.

1.9.1. Example of a Case: Iron Ox (USA)

Iron Ox manages planting, harvesting, and fertilizer distribution in greenhouses using AI-powered robots and self-sufficient hydroponic systems. Every day, their farms modify their growth patterns in response to sensor data and AI prediction algorithms.

Prospects for the Future:

- Precision horticulture and large-scale monoculture will be able to succeed with zero-human-intervention farming;
- Farmers will increasingly take on the role of farm system engineers, managing digital twins of their operations instead of operating tractors.

1.9.2. Climate Resilience Powered by AI

AI as a Protector against Climate Change

AI will be the most effective protection against agriculture's biggest challenge, which is the climate problem. Cutting-edge algorithms are able to precisely provide adaptive tactics, rethink cropping systems, and simulate various climate scenarios.

Applications Include:

- **Crop Simulation Models:** AI can model how various crop types will react to future climatic trends, such as pests, salinity, and drought.
- **Hyperlocal Weather Forecasting**: Field-level predictions with actionable alerts can be generated by machine learning algorithms trained on historical and satellite data.
- **Disaster Anticipation:** By modelling the likelihood of occurrences such as locust swarms, floods, or heat waves weeks in advance, predictive AI enables proactive measures.

1.9.2.1. Case Example: CGIAR's Climate-Smart Agriculture Platforms

CGIAR, a global agricultural research alliance, has developed AI-powered tools to assist Sub-Saharan African farmers in selecting climate-resilient crops and modifying planting windows. To customize tactics, these technologies integrate soil data, meteorological models, and socioeconomic inputs.

Long-Term Prospects: AI-generated seed types tailored to changing climate circumstances; mobile phone-based digital climate advisors that advise millions of smallholders on when, what, and how to plant.

1.9.3. International Networks for Agri-Intelligence

Transforming Remote Farms into Networked Intelligence

A global network of interconnected AI systems—sharing information, cooperating to learn, and creating a planetary-scale agri-intelligence network—is the key to the future of agriculture.

Vision:

- Using federated learning, farms on different continents exchange data, allowing for worldwide pattern recognition without sacrificing local data privacy.
- To prevent overproduction, reduce food waste, and maintain a balanced global food supply, AI collaboratives coordinate crop production across geographical boundaries.

1.9.3.1. Example: AI used with the FAO's Global Information and Early Warning System (GIEWS)

AI might help **GIEWS**, which now tracks food insecurity, become an early responder by modelling solutions in addition to identifying emergencies.

Prospective Situation: Consider an AI that detects below-normal rainfall in East Africa and sends out a warning to India to increase the cultivation of legumes in order to make up for it in the world's food supply chains. Shared agri-intelligence makes such planetary resilience possible.

1.9.4. The Emergence of Agri-Neural Interfaces (Human-AI Collaboration)

Beyond Automation: Symbiotic Intelligence

Future farmers might not only engage with AI, but also integrate cognitive skills with it as *Brain-Computer Interface* (BCI) technologies advance. Farmers would be able to visualize field health, evaluate data, and operate machines with just their thoughts thanks to agri-neural interfaces.

How it operates:

- Brain impulses are converted into commands by non-invasive neural devices, such as headbands or AR glasses.
- AI programs pick up on the farmer's decision-making habits and start offering quicker or better options.
- This collaboration enables real-time data analysis and field execution.

Use Cases Include:

- Using augmented reality to see disease outbreaks predicted by AI.
- The use of drones for spraying or surveys that are thought-activated.
- An AI that makes crop decisions in real time based on the stress levels and brain activity of farmers.

Ownership Of Neuronal Data Is One Ethical Consideration.

- Cognitive overload or an addiction to AI on a

psychological level.

- Laws governing the use of brain data in agricultural technology.

1.9.5. Concluding Remarks: Developing the Smart Agri-Future

AI is evolving into a collaborator in agriculture rather than merely a tool. *The future of farming is changing into a hyperconnected, forward-thinking ecosystem, driven by everything from neural augmentation and global intelligence networks to predictive systems and autonomous farms.* However, this shift necessitates inclusive innovation, strong ethics, fair access, and imaginative policy—or else it runs the risk of making the same issues AI is meant to address worse.

The future of agriculture, as this chapter has demonstrated, is a drastic shift driven by artificial intelligence rather than a continuation of existing patterns. The combination of global intelligence systems, deep learning, robots, and neural interfaces portends a time when agriculture is:

- **Climate-Resilient** as opposed to vulnerable;
- **Autonomous** as opposed to labour-intensive;
- **Collaborative And Planetary** as opposed to compartmentalized and regional;
- **Neuro-integrated**, augmenting human understanding with machine speed and precision;

Unprecedented resilience, sustainability, and productivity are made possible by each of these developments. However, these exponential capacities come with equally significant responsibilities: to maintain the accessibility, morality, and inclusivity of these technologies.

1.9.6. Last Words of Advice

- **For Policymakers:** By funding open data platforms, AI literacy initiatives, and rural connections, you must provide the digital basis. *Establish legal frameworks that protect privacy, land rights, and moral principles while promoting innovation.* Everyone should have access to AI; it shouldn't be a privilege of a select few.
- **For Innovators & Tech Companies:** The goal isn't only to build better machines, but to *create farmer-first ecosystems.* Create AI tools that are linguistically localized, intuitive, and resource-efficient. Include participatory design, which requires farmers to co-design the systems they will utilize.
- **For Farmers:** In today's digital world, farmers are more than just landowners; they are also data scientists, systems administrators, and decision-makers. *Accept lifelong learning. Demand control over your data and openness. Adopt new tools with courage, but use caution when depending too heavily on automation.*
- **For International Organizations:** Make sure AI is used to promote global food justice. Instead of only responding to hunger, *use AI-enhanced networks and predictive food systems to avoid and predict it.* Encourage international cooperation in AI to preserve biodiversity and balance food systems.

1.9.7. The Way Forward

The future of agriculture is being *shaped by brainwaves, biosensors, satellites, and algorithms*. The ink is still wet, though. We have the ability—and the duty—to control how these technologies will affect the fate of our food systems, the health of our planet, and the lives of billions of people.

Let's make sure AI in agriculture is wise, not just intelligent.

In summary, *the seed has been sown. Agriculture 4.0 is becoming a reality rather than a sci-fi idea. Data scientists are emerging from farmers. Fields are becoming into ecosystems with intelligence. Additionally, food—one of humanity's most basic needs—is being produced in more sustainable, intelligent, and clean ways than ever before.*

We'll go into great detail about this change in the upcoming chapters, covering everything from the AI models that schedule every drop of water to the algorithms that forecast crop yields to the autonomous tractors that till fields. AI in agriculture has entered a new era. The future is being farmed.

Chapter 2: Comprehending Precision Farming

2.1. Precision Farming: What is it?

Precision farming, sometimes referred to as *Precision Agriculture, is a contemporary farming management approach that maximizes crop yield and resource utilization via the use of technology, data, and analytics.* Precision farming acknowledges that distinct areas of a field have different needs—such as varying soil fertility, moisture, or pest pressure—and manages them accordingly rather than treating entire fields evenly.

In order to collect data in real time, this method *integrates cutting-edge technologies such as GPS-guided machinery, drones, satellite imaging, soil sensors, weather forecasting, and AI-powered analytics.* Following that, farmers can decide how best to plant, water, fertilize, and control pests at each place.

By using the appropriate input at the appropriate time, location, and quantity, precision farming aims to maximize yields, decrease waste, cut production costs, and lessen its negative effects on the environment.

To put it briefly, precision farming—often referred to as a core pillar of agriculture—converts conventional agriculture from a homogenous, haphazard practice into a data-driven, extremely effective, and sustainable system. 4.0.

2.1.1. Essential Elements of Precision Agriculture

1. **Geographic Information Systems (GIS) and Global Positioning Systems (GPS)**

- Accurate position tracking for planting, spraying, and harvesting is made possible by GPS technology.

    1. **Drones & Remote Sensing**

- To identify agricultural stress, insect infestations, and growth patterns, satellites and drones take pictures from the air.
- Farmers can keep an eye on plant health with multispectral and hyper-spectral imaging long before issues become apparent to the human eye.

    1. **Crop and Soil Sensors**

- Real-time measurements of temperature, pH, nutrient levels, and soil moisture are possible.
- Assist in identifying the precise input needs for every field section.

    1. **Variable Rate Technology (VRT)**

- Equipment that uses data inputs to automatically modify the rate at which pesticides are sprayed, fertilizer is applied, or seeds are planted.
- Assures that every region receives precisely what it requires, neither more nor less.

    1. **Machine Learning And Artificial Intelligence**

- AI recommends the best farming practices by analysing vast datasets from sensors, drones, and historical records.

- Yield results, pest outbreaks, and irrigation requirements are predicted by predictive algorithms.

1. **Platforms for Data Management**

- Data from all sources is gathered, saved, and examined by cloud-based farm management software.
- Enables farmers to make decisions, see trends, and monitor development over time.

1. **Robotics and Automated Machinery**

- With little assistance from humans, autonomous tractors, harvesters, and planters operate precisely.
- Robots are highly accurate at repeated activities like picking fruit or weeding.

2.1.2. Advantages of Precision Farming

1. **A Rise In Crop Yields**

- Crops receive the best care possible when farming methods are customized to meet the particular requirements of each plot, which raises productivity and improves yield quality.

    1. **Lower Input Expenses**

- Accurate seed, fertilizer, pesticide, and water application reduces waste and operating costs.

    1. **Increased Resource Efficiency**

- To ensure optimal efficiency, farmers can apply the appropriate input at the appropriate time, location, and quantity.

    1. **Ecological Sustainability**

- Water contamination and soil deterioration are less likely when excessive fertilizer and pesticide use is reduced.
- Promotes biodiversity-preserving regenerative agricultural methods.

    1. **Improved Choice-Making**

- Predictive analytics and real-time data enable farmers to make well-informed decisions rather of depending solely on tradition or conjecture.

    1. **Climate Resilience**

- AI-powered forecasting aids farmers in becoming ready for disease threats, insect outbreaks, and harsh weather.
- Precision irrigation avoids overwatering in wet seasons and conserves water during droughts.

    1. **Higher Profit Margins**

- Farmers can make more money when they increase yields,

reduce input costs, and improve product quality.

1. **Labour Optimization**

- Robotics and automation lessen reliance on human labour for dangerous or repetitive jobs.

1. **Market Competitiveness**

- Farmers can satisfy the high quality requirements set by international markets thanks to data-driven farming.

2.1.3. Difficulties in Putting Precision Farming into Practice

1. **High Initial Investment**

- It can be costly, particularly for smallholder farmers, to buy sensors, drones, GPS-enabled equipment, and AI-powered software.

    1. **Technical Proficiency Gap**

- In areas with low technical literacy, farmers may find it difficult to operate sophisticated machinery and decipher complicated data without training.

    1. **Data Management Overload**

- Precision farming produces vast amounts of data that need to be securely stored, analysed, and incorporated into choices.

    1. **Connectivity Problems**

- Cloud-based farm management solutions require dependable internet access, yet connectivity is frequently inadequate in rural regions.

    1. **Maintenance and Upkeep Costs**

- Regular maintenance is necessary for equipment like automated tractors, drones, and sensors, which raises operating expenses.

    1. **System Interoperability**:

- Data integration might be difficult due to incompatibilities between various precision farming instruments and platforms.

    1. **Risk of Technology Dependence**

- Farmers who rely too much on technology may be more susceptible to interruptions from software bugs, cyberattacks, or power outages.

1. **Unequal Access to Technology**

- The productivity gap is growing as wealthier commercial farms adopt precision agriculture more quickly than small-scale farmers.

1. **Regulatory and Data Privacy Issues**

- Ownership, privacy, and the moral use of information are issues that arise when agricultural data is shared with service providers.

2.1.4. AI's Function in Accurate Farming

The technology that propels precision farming from data collecting to data-driven decision-making is artificial intelligence (AI). AI transforms the massive quantities of data from these instruments into useful insights, whereas traditional precision agriculture depends on hardware such as sensors, drones, and GPS equipment.

1. **Crop Yield Predictive Analytics**

- AI algorithms anticipate yields with high accuracy by analysing previous weather, soil, and crop data.
- To maximize yield, farmers might modify planting schedules, input amounts, and harvest times.

    1. **Identification of Disease and Pests**

- Using drone and satellite data, AI-powered picture recognition finds early indicators of disease or pest infestation.
- Reduces the need for pesticides by enabling focused treatment before issues worsen.

    1. **Intelligent Systems for Irrigation**

- To automate irrigation schedules, machine learning algorithms analyse crop water requirements, soil moisture, and weather forecasts.
- Prevents excessive or insufficient irrigation and minimizes water waste.

    1. **Optimization of Variable Rate Input**

- AI blends multispectral imaging, soil data, and agricultural development trends to predict the exact number of seeds, fertilizers, and pesticides for each region of the field.

1. **Guidance for Autonomous Machinery**

- AI is used by self-driving tractors and robotic harvesters to navigate, recognize obstacles, and complete tasks with little assistance from humans.

1. **Climate Risk Management**

- AI algorithms forecast severe weather conditions and recommend flexible approaches to save livestock and crops.

1. **Supply Chain and Market Optimization**

- AI helps farmers choose the best time and location to sell their produce in order to maximize profits by analysing market demand, commodity prices, and logistical variables.

1. **Continuous Learning Systems**

- AI models get better with each season by learning from fresh farm data, increasing the accuracy of their forecasts and suggestions.

2.2. What Are Intelligent Watering Systems?

Smart irrigation systems are cutting-edge water management technologies that deliver the exact amount of water required by crops at the proper time and location by utilizing technology, automation, and data analytics. Smart irrigation adjusts in real time based on crop type, development stage, weather patterns, and soil moisture, in contrast to traditional irrigation techniques that frequently follow set schedules regardless of the actual field conditions.

To guarantee the best possible water use, these systems integrate sensors, artificial intelligence (AI) algorithms, Internet of Things (IoT) devices, and automated controls. Smart irrigation is a crucial part of precision farming and climate-resilient agriculture because it increases crop yields, decreases water waste, and improves sustainability.

2.2.1. Important Characteristics of Intelligent Irrigation Systems

1. **Soil Moisture Sensors:** Determine when irrigation is actually required by measuring the soil's water content.
2. **Weather-Based Controls:** Using previous climate data and current weather forecasts, modify watering schedules.
3. **AI-Powered Decision Making:** Evaluate various data sources to suggest or schedule irrigation schedules for every crop zone.
4. **Variable Rate Irrigation (VRI):** Depending on the needs of the soil and the crops, variable rate irrigation (VRI) distributes varying amounts of water to various areas of the field.
5. **Remote Monitoring and Control:** From any location, farmers may use a computer or smartphone to monitor and modify irrigation settings.
6. **Integration with Other Systems:** For comprehensive farm management, it coordinates with systems for pest control, fertilizer, and precision planting.

Benefits Include:

- Significant water savings, frequently between 30 and 50 percent.
- Increased crop quality and output.
- Lower labour and operating expenses.
- Reduced environmental effect by using water responsibly.

2.2.2. Smart Irrigation System Types

1. **Climate-Smart (Weather-Based) Irrigation Controllers**

- Also known as Evapotranspiration (ET) Controllers, these devices modify watering schedules in response to local meteorological information, including as wind speed, temperature, humidity, and sun radiation.
- They determine the pace at which water seeps from plants and evaporates from the soil, making sure irrigation only occurs when required.

    1. **Sensor Systems for Soil Moisture**

- To determine the true water content of the soil at various levels, use in-field probes.
- The irrigation system only turns on when the crop's moisture content falls below ideal levels.

    1. **Intelligent Controls for Drip Irrigation**

- Through a system of pipelines and emitters managed by timers, sensors, or artificial intelligence algorithms, water is delivered straight to the root zone.
- Reduces water loss through runoff or evaporation, making it perfect for high-value crops, vineyards, and orchards.

    1. **Lateral Movement and Centre Pivot Intelligent Systems**

- Large-scale automated irrigation systems that have been improved using real-time data integration, variable rate technology (VRT), and GPS guidance.
- Has the ability to administer varying amounts of water to various fields in a single irrigation pass.

1. **Subsurface Drip Irrigation (SDI):**

- This technique lowers evaporation and inhibits the growth of weeds by placing drip lines beneath the soil's surface to supply water straight to plant roots.
- For precise fertigation, they are frequently combined with nutrient injection devices.

1. **Autonomous Irrigation Robots Driven by AI**

- Mobile irrigation devices that autonomously traverse fields while instantly assessing crop and soil requirements.
- Especially helpful for particular crop systems and high-tech greenhouses.

1. **IoT-Integrated Sprinkler Systems**

- To maximize water utilization and spray patterns, conventional sprinklers have been enhanced with IoT sensors and wireless controls.

2.2.3. AI's Function in Intelligent Irrigation Systems

Irrigation is changing from a manual, schedule-based activity to a completely automated, adaptable, and predictive operation thanks to artificial intelligence. AI makes sure that every drop of water is used as efficiently as possible by combining real-time sensor data, weather forecasts, crop growth models, and past farm records.

1. **Water Demand Predictive Modelling**

- AI algorithms use soil type, development stage, and predicted weather to predict a crop's future water requirements.
- Reduces crop stress by preventing both overwatering and underwatering.

   1. **Automated Irrigation Scheduling**

- Without human input, AI systems decide when and how much water to apply.
- Schedules are continuously modified by these systems in response to fresh data.

   1. **Integration with Sensor Networks and the Internet of Things**

- AI generates a dynamic irrigation plan by analysing data from weather stations, drones, and soil moisture monitors.
- Reacts immediately to modifications in the atmospheric or soil conditions.

   1. **Variable Rate Irrigation Optimization:**

- AI-driven controls adjust water content in a field based on soil capacity and plant requirements.

1. **Leak and Fault Detection**

- By identifying irregularities in water pressure or flow, machine learning models can find leaks or clogged emitters early on, preventing water loss.

1. **Climatic Resilience Planning**:

- AI is able to simulate long-term climatic trends and recommend irrigation plans that adjust to floods, droughts, or changing seasons of precipitation.

1. **Fertigation Management:**

- AI systems make sure that fertilizers are administered at the proper times and concentrations for optimal absorption by coordinating irrigation and nutrient delivery.

1. **Continuous System Learning**

- AI improves its recommendations every season by gradually learning the unique behaviour of a farm's soil, crops, and microclimate.

2.3. What Are Crop Prediction Systems?

Crop prediction systems are cutting-edge technical solutions that estimate crop growth, yield, and quality prior to harvest by utilizing data analytics, *Artificial Intelligence (AI), Machine Learning (ML),* and remote sensing. To produce precise, data-driven insights, these systems examine enormous datasets, ranging from past crop performance and insect activity to weather and soil characteristics.

Helping farmers, agribusinesses, and governments predict output levels, allocate resources optimally, and reduce risks well in advance is the main objective. Crop prediction is a strategic decision-making technique that converts uncertainty into useful information in the context of precision agriculture.

2.3.1. Important Sources of Information for Crop Prediction Systems:

1. **Normalized Difference Vegetation Index (NDVI):** Plant health, development stages, and vegetation indicators like the *Normalized Difference Vegetation Index (NDVI)* are tracked by satellite and drone imagery.
2. **Soil Data:** Details about the pH, moisture content, texture, and nutrient makeup of the soil.
3. **Weather Data:** Current forecasts and historical climatic records are used to evaluate growth circumstances.
4. **Crop Models** are mathematical representations of how particular crops react to management and environmental influences.
5. **Reports on diseases and pests:** These are early alerts about dangers that can reduce productivity.
6. **Farm Management Records:** Previous fertilizer applications, planting dates, and irrigation plans.

Crop prediction systems are used in the following applications:

- **Yield Forecasting**, which estimates harvest amounts to plan market, storage, and transportation strategies.
- **Market planning:** Match supply and demand to keep prices stable and prevent gluts or shortages.
- **Risk management:** Get ready for possible crop failures brought on by pest outbreaks, floods, or drought.
- **Resource Optimization:** Make better use of labour, fertilizer, and water.
- **Policy and Food Security:** To inform national food

security plans, governments and non-governmental organizations use aggregated forecasts.

2.3.2. Artificial Intelligence in Crop Prediction Systems

Crop prediction systems can be made more accurate and efficient with the help of *Artificial Intelligence (AI).* Artificial Intelligence (AI) systems can find patterns and produce forecasts that are significantly more accurate than those produced by conventional approaches by digesting complex and varied facts.

1. **Integration and Analysis of Data**

- AI algorithms generate a comprehensive picture of crop health and growth circumstances by combining data from sensors, drones, satellites, and historical records.

    1. **Machine Learning for Yield Forecasting**

- Machine learning algorithms forecast yields under various conditions by learning from historical crop performance and environmental parameters.

    1. **Early Risk Identification**

- AI-powered image identification enables prompt interventions by seeing early indicators of illnesses, insect infestations, or vitamin deficits.

    1. **Weather Impact Modelling:**

- AI models how various weather patterns affect crop growth, allowing farmers to make proactive management adjustments.

    1. **Tailored Suggestions**

- AI systems may provide farmers with recommendations on the best times to plant, when to water, and how much fertilizer to use for their particular fields based on projections.

    1. **Continuous Learning and Improvement:**

- As fresh data becomes available, AI models revise their forecasts, increasing their accuracy over time and adjusting to shifting climatic conditions.

1. **Supply Chain Optimization**

- AI helps stakeholders plan logistics, storage, and market distribution effectively by predicting production numbers.

In conclusion, artificial intelligence (AI) turns crop prediction from a reactive guesswork exercise into a proactive, accurate, and data-driven approach that is crucial to the sustainability and financial success of modern agriculture.

2.4. Self-Driving Tractors: Transforming Farm Equipment

A significant advancement in farm mechanization, autonomous tractors use robotics, GPS, and artificial intelligence (AI) to carry out farming duties with little to no assistance from humans. These autonomous vehicles have the ability to precisely and efficiently plough, plant, spray, and harvest crops, revolutionizing farm operations.

2.4.1. Autonomous Tractors' salient features include:

1. **GPS and RTK Positioning**

- To navigate fields with centimetre-level accuracy, use Real-Time Kinematic (RTK) and Global Positioning System (GPS) technologies.

1. **AI-Assisted Decision-Making and Navigation**

- Tractors are guided by AI algorithms that use real-time field data to optimize routes, avoid obstacles, and modify operations.

1. **Sensor Integration**

- Outfitted with cameras, LiDAR, and ultrasonic sensors to identify barriers, crop conditions, and terrain characteristics.

1. **Remote Monitoring and Control**

- Using computers or cellphones, farmers can remotely monitor and control tractor operations.

1. **Safety Features**

- To guarantee safe operation, autonomous tractors come equipped with fail-safes, obstacle detection, and emergency stop features.

2.4.2. Advantages of Autonomous Tractor:

- **Enhanced Efficiency:** Maximize field coverage by working longer hours with reliable performance.
- **Lower Labour Costs:** Address labour shortages and reduce reliance on experienced operators.
- **Precision Operations:** Reduce crop damage and input waste by carrying out farming chores with extreme precision.
- **Enhanced Safety:** Reduce human exposure to dangerous situations or physically demanding tasks.
- **Data Collection:** To help guide precision farming decisions, collect field data continuously.

2.4.3. Challenges:

- **High Initial Costs:** Purchasing and maintaining cutting-edge technology can be costly.
- **Technical Complexity:** Operation and troubleshooting need for qualified staff.
- **Legal and Regulatory Concerns**: Autonomous equipment brings up issues with safety regulations and liabilities.

To sum up, autonomous tractors are essential components of contemporary, intelligent agriculture, boosting output and assisting farmers in resource management.

2.5. Crop Monitoring Powered by AI

In order to deliver constant, real-time insights into crop health, growth, and stress factors, AI-driven crop monitoring combines artificial intelligence with sensor technologies, drones, and satellite imaging. With this method, farmers can identify problems early, maximize inputs, and enhance crop management in general for increased yields and sustainability.

2.5.1. Important Elements of AI-Powered Crop Monitoring:

1. **Technologies for Remote Sensing**

- Take detailed pictures of crop fields using satellites and drones fitted with thermal, hyper spectral, and multispectral sensors.
- These pictures show details that are not visible to the human eye, like illness symptoms, water stress, and chlorophyll levels.

    1. **Sensor Networks**

- In various field zones, ground-based sensors record temperature, nutrient levels, soil moisture, and microclimate variables.

    1. **Automated Notifications and Suggestions**

- When anomalies are found, systems alert farmers right away and suggest exact actions like irrigation or focused spraying.

    1. **Historical Data Integration**

- Tracks trends in crop development and enhances prediction accuracy over time by combining recent observations with historical data.

    1. **Scalable Platforms**

- Farmers of various sizes can access monitoring data remotely using computers or cellphones thanks to cloud-based interfaces.

    1. **Image Analysis and Machine Learning**

- Artificial intelligence algorithms examine sensor data and images to find trends and discover early indicators of diseases, pests, or nutrient shortages.
- Provides very accurate distinction between stressed and

healthy plants.

1. **Benefits:**

- Reduces agricultural losses by facilitating early problem discovery.
- Promotes accurate water, fertilizer, and pesticide application, reducing waste and its negative effects on the environment.
- Enhances harvest planning and yield forecasting.
- Saves time and personnel expenses by eliminating the need for manual field inspections.
- Improves decision-making by providing practical insights based on actual data.

2.6. Agriculture Using AI and Machine Learning Models

Farmers and agribusinesses can now evaluate complex data and make better decisions thanks to artificial intelligence (AI) and machine learning (ML) models, which have become essential tools in modern agriculture. To forecast results, optimize inputs, and improve crop management, these models analyse enormous volumes of data from sensors, satellites, weather stations, and historical records.

2.6.1. AI and ML Model Types Frequently Employed in Agriculture:

1. **Models of Supervised Learning**

- Train algorithms for tasks including yield prediction, disease detection, and crop categorization using labelled datasets.
- Neural networks, Random Forest, and *Support Vector Machines* (SVM) are a few examples.

    1. **Unsupervised Learning Models**

- Find hidden patterns or groups in data without labels; these are helpful for detecting anomalies or clustering soil types.
- **Examples** include *Principal Component Analysis* (PCA) and K-means clustering.

    1. **Reinforcement Learning**

- Robotics and autonomous machinery navigation benefit from algorithms that learn the best course of action through interaction with the environment.

    1. **Deep Learning**

- Employ multi-layered neural networks to evaluate intricate picture data for applications such as identifying pests or evaluating the health of plants.
- **Example**: *Convolutional Neural Networks* (CNNs) are one example.

    1. **Models for Predictive Analytics**

- Use both historical and current data to forecast agricultural yields, insect outbreaks, and climatic consequences.

    1. **Uses in Agriculture:**

- **Disease and Pest Detection:** Using image analysis to identify diseases early.
- **Precision Irrigation:** Using predictive models to optimize water use is known as precision irrigation.
- **Yield Forecasting:** In order to organize the supply chain, yield forecasting involves estimating production volumes.
- **Soil Health Monitoring:** Predicting nutrient deficits and the likelihood of soil degradation is possible through soil health monitoring.
- **Autonomous Farm Equipment:** Facilitating task optimization and navigation.

1. **Advantages:**

- Increased precision in decision-making.
- Improved sustainability and resource efficiency.
- A decrease in operating expenses and crop losses.
- The capacity to scale insights across various farm sizes and geographical areas.

2.7. AI's Obstacles and Prospects in Agriculture

There are still a number of issues that need to be resolved as AI technologies continue to disrupt agriculture, but there are also promising new developments that could further alter farming methods.

2.7.1. Challenges:

1. **Availability and Quality of Data**

- A lot of farms lack the reliable, high-quality data needed to build AI models that work.
- Sensors and digital tools are frequently inaccessible to smallholder farmers.

    1. **Expensive Expenses And Infrastructure Needs**

- Particularly in developing nations, initial expenditures for AI hardware, software, and connection may be exorbitant.
- Many AI systems require dependable electricity and internet.

    1. **Technical Expertise Gap**

- To implement and sustain AI technologies, farmers and agricultural workers require training.
- Specialists with knowledge of both agronomy and artificial intelligence are in short supply.

    1. **Interoperability and Integration**

- Distinct AI hardware and platforms frequently function in isolation, making data exchange and coordinated decision-making more difficult.

    1. **Ownership of Data and Privacy**

- There are still unanswered questions about farm data ownership and usage, which raise moral and legal issues.

    1. **Impact on the Environment and Society**

- An over-reliance on AI may aggravate disparities between large and small farms and marginalize traditional knowledge.

2.7.2. Trends for the Future:

1. **Edge AI and IoT Growth**

- AI processing is increasingly taking place on edge devices, such as drones and sensors, which lowers latency and eliminates reliance on cloud connectivity.

    1. **AI-Driven Robotics**

- Development of self-governing robots that can carry out intricate operations like planting, weeding, and selective harvesting.

    1. **Genomics and AI Integration**

- In order to develop crops that are suited for certain environments, AI models will progressively integrate genetic and environmental data.

    1. **Blockchain and AI for Transparency**

- Using blockchain and AI together to improve food safety, traceability, and fair trade verification.

    1. **Collaborative AI Platforms**

- By bridging the digital gap, shared, open-source AI tools will enable farmers all around the world to access cutting-edge technologies.

    1. **Climate-Smart AI Solutions**

- Through resilient crop planning and predictive analytics, AI will be more involved in assisting agriculture in adapting to climate change.

    1. **Personalized Farming Recommendations**

- AI will offer hyper-local, farmer-specific guidance after carefully examining farmer preferences and agricultural conditions.

2.8. Synopsis and Important Lessons for Integrating AI and Precision Agriculture

Artificial Intelligence (AI)-powered precision agriculture is revolutionizing farming by facilitating more intelligent, effective, and sustainable agricultural production. *Farmers can precisely manage their fields to maximize yields and minimize waste by integrating cutting-edge technologies like GPS, sensors, drones, and AI-powered analytics.*

Key Takeaways:

- **Precision Farming** improves production and environmental results by customizing inputs like water, fertilizer, and herbicides to the unique requirements of various field zones using data and technology.
- **Smart Irrigation Systems** greatly reduce water consumption and promote climate resilience by automating and optimizing water use using sensors, weather data, and artificial intelligence.
- AI is used by **Crop Prediction Systems** to predict yields, identify illnesses early, and direct resource allocation, lowering risks and increasing profitability.
- **Robotics and Autonomous Tractors** automate field operations, boosting productivity, lowering labour costs, and guaranteeing constant accuracy.
- Real-time insights into crop health are provided by **AI-Driven Crop Monitoring**, enabling proactive management that maximizes inputs and reduces losses.
- **Challenges** - To guarantee fair access and successful AI deployment in agriculture, issues such high costs, data

quality, connectivity, and talent gaps must be resolved.

- **Trends for the future** suggest that AI technology will become more accessible, integrated, and climate-smart, further revolutionizing farming methods around the world.

A vital route to sustainably feeding the world's expanding population, enhancing farmers' livelihoods, and safeguarding natural resources for coming generations is the combination of AI and precision agriculture.

2.9. Case Study 1: Digital Green Initiative in India

A non-profit organization called **Digital Green** employs AI-powered warnings based on local field data and satellite imaging in rural India, where 85% of farms are smaller than two hectares. WhatsApp videos in regional dialects provide farmers with individualized advice on when to plant, water, and harvest.

Findings:

- A 10%–15% improvement in yield.
- A 20% reduction in input.
- A greater use of environmentally beneficial methods

2.10. Case Study 2: Bayer's Climate FieldView

Large-scale farms can obtain comprehensive zone-by-zone analysis using **Climate FieldView**, a commercial precision agriculture platform that integrates satellite imagery, soil mapping, weather forecasts, and machine data.

Important AI Features:

- AI-guided fungicide application timing;
- Interactive field health maps using NDVI;
- Hybrid and field yield forecast

Result:

- A 5–10% increase in average yield.
- A notable decrease in crop loss as a result of prompt disease notifications.

2.10.1. Diagram: Benefits of Precision Agriculture

Category	**Benefit**
Productivity	Increased production per acre by using inputs optimally.
Profitability	Input cost are reduced while margins are increased.
Sustainability	Lower emissions and resource conservation.
Risk Reduction	Crop failure rates are detected early.
Customisation	Every micro zone of a field has specific strategies

Figure 2: Benefits of Precision Agriculture

2.11. Challenges with Adoption

Adoption of PA confronts a number of obstacles despite its potential:

- The price of entry for platforms and sensors.
- The disparity in smallholder farmers' digital literacy.
- Data silos brought on by platforms that are incompatible.
- Problems with connectivity in rural places.
- Issues with ownership and privacy around farm data.

Government subsidies, open-source platforms, farmer cooperatives, and mobile-first solutions are all being used to address these issues.

2.12. Prospects for the Future: Precision 2.0

The following will be the next generation of precision farmers:

- **Predictive:** Simulating outcomes based on climate change models using artificial intelligence.
- **Prescriptive:** Providing detailed plans of action rather than merely insights.
- **Completely Self-Sufficient:** using robotics for complete automation.
- **Decentralized:** Blockchain-powered for data ownership and traceability.
- **Collaborative:** Using common platforms to link farmers, researchers, agribusinesses, and legislators.

Example: Precision for Regenerative Agriculture In the future, PA will prioritize improving biodiversity, lowering carbon emissions, and restoring soil health over yield maximization alone. AI will monitor soil carbon, recommend cover crops, and direct rotational grazing, transforming sustainability from an ethical to a fundamental business objective.

In conclusion, Precision farming is becoming a need rather than a luxury. AI-powered precision systems provide a route to resilience and profitability as farmers negotiate the challenges of contemporary agriculture—changing customer expectations, fluctuating weather, and growing expenses. One of the most fascinating applications of AI in agriculture will be discussed in the upcoming chapter: crop prediction, a field in which data science and machine learning are assisting farmers in knowing what will be harvested tomorrow.

Chapter 3: Crop Prediction Based on Science

3.1. Why Crop Prediction Is Important

Because it empowers farmers, agribusinesses, and policymakers to make well-informed decisions, crop prediction is essential to modern agriculture. Precise predictions of agricultural yields and growth trends contribute to waste reduction, resource optimization, and increased production. Crop forecast is significant for the following main reasons:

3.1.1. **Better Resource Management and Planning**

Farmers can more efficiently arrange planting, irrigation, fertilizing, and harvesting when they can forecast crop yields. By reducing the misuse or underuse of resources like labour, fertilizer, and water, this improves environmental sustainability and lowers costs.

3.1.2. **Food Security and Risk Mitigation**

Crop prediction aids in anticipating either shortages or abundant harvests. Early warnings improve food security and stabilize market prices by allowing governments and groups to plan for food shortages or surpluses.

3.1.3. **Supply Chain and Market Optimization**

Reducing post-harvest losses and guaranteeing timely produce delivery to markets are two benefits of using accurate crop predictions to help supply chain partners arrange storage, transportation, and distribution more effectively.

3.1.4. **Adaptation and Resilience to Climate Change**

Crop prediction models that incorporate weather data assist farmers in adapting their operations to changing conditions, thereby decreasing their susceptibility to pests, floods, and droughts, as climate variability affects agriculture.

3.1.5. **Facilitating the Integration of AI and Precision Agriculture**

A key component of precision agriculture is crop prediction, in which data analytics and artificial intelligence (AI) optimize farming choices at the micro level to maximize yields while reducing environmental effect.

3.2. The Data That Backs Up the Forecast

A vast array of data and information gathered from multiple sources is necessary for accurate crop forecast. *Predictive models and algorithms use this data to forecast yields by analysing crop growth patterns.* The following are important categories of data that aid in crop prediction:

3.2.1. **Weather Information**

Crop growth is significantly impacted by weather factors as temperature, humidity, wind speed, rainfall, and sun radiation. Weather data from the past and present can be used to identify hazards like frost or drought and forecast how crops will grow throughout a growing season.

3.2.2. **Information on Soil**

Crop health and yield potential are influenced by soil properties such as texture, pH, organic matter, moisture content, and nutrient concentration. Sensor data and routine soil testing are crucial inputs for crop growth models.

3.2.3. **Type and Variety of Crops**

Within a crop species, different crops and even variations have different growing needs, productivity potentials, and susceptibility to disease. Accurate forecast depends on knowing the precise crop type.

3.2.4. **Data from Satellites and Remote Sensing**

Large-scale, current views of crop health, canopy cover, and biomass are provided via satellite photography and drone data. Monitoring crop growth and identifying stressors like pests or nutrient shortages are made possible by these remote sensing technologies.

3.2.5. **Records of Historical Yield**

In order to calibrate models and comprehend long-term patterns caused by environmental and management factors, historical yield data from particular fields or areas serve as a baseline.

3.2.6. **Procedures for Management**

Crop growth is directly impacted by information regarding planting dates, irrigation schedules, fertilizer programs, pest control methods, and crop rotation techniques.

3.2.7. **Incidence of Disease and Pests**

By accounting for possible yield losses, tracking pest and disease outbreaks helps prediction models.

3.2.8. **Land Use and Terrain**

Elevation and slope are two examples of terrain characteristics that affect agricultural productivity by influencing microclimates and water drainage.

By combining these many data sources with AI and advanced analytics, crop projections become more accurate and dependable, enabling stakeholders to maximize agricultural results.

3.3. Predicting Pests and Crop Disease

A key element of contemporary crop prediction systems is the ability to forecast crop diseases and pest outbreaks. *Farmers can minimize crop losses and lessen the need for excessive chemical use by taking quick, targeted action when these threats are identified and predicted early.* Important elements consist of:

3.3.1. The Value of Disease and Pest Forecasting

Pests and diseases can drastically lower crop quality and production. By facilitating early action, forecasting helps prevent widespread infestations, protecting food output and farmers' profits.

3.3.2. Sources of Forecasting Data

- **Climate and Weather Information:** Certain climatic factors, like humidity, temperature, and rainfall, are ideal for the growth of numerous diseases and pests. Fungal illnesses, for instance, frequently spread quickly in warm, humid conditions.
- **Remote Sensing and Imaging:** Before obvious signs show up, satellite and drone photography can identify changes in crop health that could point to the presence of pests or diseases.
- **Field Sensors:** Real-time information about the emergence of pests and diseases can be obtained from sensors that track temperature, soil moisture, and plant health.
- **Historical Outbreak Records:** Information from previous disease and pest outbreaks can be used to forecast the probability and timing of future occurrences.

3.3.3. AI Methods and Predictive Models

Advanced models evaluate gathered data and predict epidemics using statistical and machine learning methods. To calculate the risk level, these models take into account variables like environmental conditions, host crop sensitivity, and pest life cycles.

3.3.4. Advantages of Predicting

- **Targeted Intervention:** By using biological controls or pesticides just where and when necessary, farmers can lower expenses and their impact on the environment.
- **Better Crop Health:** Plant vigour and yield potential are maintained through early diagnosis.
- **Sustainability:** Encourages integrated pest management (IPM) techniques and reduces excessive chemical use.

3.3.5. Forecasting System Examples

- **Disease Warning Systems:** Websites that notify farmers of the possibility of illnesses like mildew, blight, or rust.
- **Pest Monitoring Networks:** Programs that monitor insect populations, such as aphids or locusts, in order to predict outbreaks.

Better food security is ensured by agriculture being more robust, effective, and sustainable through the integration of disease and pest forecasting into crop prediction.

One of the most useful uses of artificial intelligence in contemporary agriculture is crop prediction. Precise projections aid in:

- Better planning by farmers (planting, fertilizing, harvesting);
- Government preparation for import/export choices or food security;
- Agribusinesses streamline their supplier networks.
- Financial firms provide performance-linked loans; insurance companies evaluate risk exposure.
- Fundamentally, crop prediction makes use of AI and machine learning to forecast yield, quality, and timeliness prior to harvest by utilizing a variety of data sources.

3.3.6. Diagram: Crop Prediction Based on Science

Figure 3: Crop Prediction Based on Science

3.4. The Information Supporting the Prediction

The strength of AI's prediction ability depends on the quality of the data it uses. Generally, crop prediction systems use a mix of the following:

3.4.1. Historical Yield Data

- Annual yield outcomes by crop and location
- Patterns of agricultural rotation and land use

3.4.2. Weather Information

- Temperature, humidity, rainfall, and solar radiation
- Past patterns and immediate projections

3.4.3. Information on Soil Health and Nutrients

- pH, phosphorus, nitrogen, and organic matter concentration
- Compaction, drainage, and texture of the soil

3.4.4. Drone And Satellite Photography

- Multispectral and NDVI imagery for vegetative health
- Detection of pest distribution, flowering stage, and canopy density

3.4.5. Sensor and Internet of Things Data

- Current field-level conditions derived from climate and moisture sensors

3.4.6. Methods

- Schedules for pesticides and fertilizers, as well as irrigation records
- A range of crops and planting techniques

3.5. AI Methods for Predicting Crops

AI-based crop prediction is a combination of several cutting-edge methods rather than depending on just one:

3.5.1. **Machine Learning:** Algorithms for *Machine Learning* (ML), including gradient boosting trees, random forests, and *Support Vector Machines* (SVM), are applied to multivariate datasets in order to categorize and forecast yield levels. For instance, an ML model might discover how Zambian maize yield is affected by nitrogen levels and rainfall.

3.5.2. **Deep Learning:** For image-based predictions, *Convolutional Neural Networks* (CNNs) are specifically utilized. CNNs forecast crop vigour, disease stress, or biomass accumulation by analysing satellite and drone data.

3.5.3. **Time-Series Forecasting:** In order to forecast harvest dates or stressful times, methods such as *Long Short-Term Memory* (LSTM) neural networks are employed to model temporal patterns in weather, soil moisture, or crop development.

3.5.4. **Geographical AI: I**dentifies zones of high/low productivity or disease breakout risk by using *Machine Learning* (ML) and *Geographic Information System* (GIS) data.

3.5.5. Case Study 1: Microsoft AI-Sowing App (India)

Microsoft and ICRISAT collaborated to create an **AI-Sowing App** for groundnut farmers in Andhra Pradesh, India:

- Farmers received SMS advisories on the best times to sow;
- The app employed AI algorithms to examine past climate and meteorological data;
- Pilot districts had a 30% boost in yield;
- Significantly lower water and fertilizer usage.

3.5.6. Study 2: OneSoil (South America, Europe, and Ukraine)

OneSoil is a crop monitoring platform driven by AI that employs satellite imagery and machine learning to:

- Recognize crop kinds;
- Forecast yields in real time; and
- Suggest management tactics tailored to a given field.

In order to improve planning and risk management across 80 million hectares worldwide, farmers can access interactive maps that include biomass trends, planting density, and health status.

3.5.7. Forecasting Crop Disease and Pests

Crop forecast includes not only how much you will grow but also potential problems.

AI programs such as Plantix, AgroScout, and PlantVillage employ machine learning and image identification to:

- Identify pest outbreaks (such as autumn armyworm, locusts) based on environmental trends;
- Identify diseases including blight, rust, and mildew.
- Set off alarms and recommend remedies before irreparable harm is done.

3.5.8. Precision Agriculture Meets Predictive Analytics

An intelligent, flexible farm management system is produced when precision agriculture and crop prediction are combined. Here's how:

3.5.8.1. Diagram: Predictive Analytics Vs Precision Agriculture

Prediction	Action Taken
Expected yield to be below trend	Delay harvesting or apply specific nutrients.
Midseason drought forecast	Schedule watering as efficiently as possible.
High disease pressure was found	Applying pesticides precisely to the areas that are affected exclusively
High-yield areas were found	Concentrate your marketing and harvesting efforts there.

Figure 4: Predictive Analytics Vs Precision Agriculture

3.5.9. Prospects for the Future

3.5.9.1. **AI-Powered Satellites For Worldwide Crop Monitoring**

Near-real-time yield projections at the national and continental levels will become commonplace as businesses like Planet Labs and Descartes Labs install satellite constellations that have been AI-analysed. This will reshape plans for humanitarian assistance and foreign trade.

3.5.9.2. **Highly Tailored Farmer Helpers**

Soon, farmers will have access to AI co-pilots that combine climatic forecasts, historical performance, and hyper-local soil data to inform every crop choice, automatically modifying forecasts as the season progresses.

3.5.9.3. **Nutritional Value Prediction**

Based on crop stress histories and maturation rates, AI may also be able to forecast quality, such as fruit sugar levels, grain protein, or even shelf life, in addition to volume.

3.5.9.4. **Predictive Contracts Supported by Blockchain**

Buyers will be able to transparently ensure future supply, lenders will be able to insure more effectively, and farmers will be able to hedge their risks thanks to smart contracts connected to crop forecasts.

3.5.10. Obstacles and Restrictions

- **Model Precision**: Biased or insufficient data can cause AI predictions to differ.
- **Access for Smallholders:** Commercial farms are the target of several prediction systems.
- **Data Privacy:** Who is the owner of the underlying data and prediction models?
- **Climate Change:** Changing climate baselines could be difficult for traditional models to handle.

Government-private sector collaborations, inclusive design, and open data standards will be necessary to meet these problems.

In conclusion, AI has transformed crop prediction from a guessing game into a science. Farmers can now look months ahead and make more informed, profitable decisions with the right data, tools, and models. Crop prediction is more than just a tool; it's the nervous system of farming in the future. In the upcoming chapter, we'll look at autonomous tractors and the future of mechanized farming, where machines not only move on their own but also think and farm more effectively than ever before.

Chapter 4: Self-Driving Tractors and the Prospects of Automated Agriculture

4.1. Why Crop Prediction Is Important

Crop prediction is essential to modern agriculture because it gives stakeholders, farmers, and policymakers insightful information that improves resource management, food security, and agricultural output. *Better decision-making is made possible by accurate crop forecasts at every stage of the farming process, from planting to harvesting and marketing.* Crop forecast is crucial for the following main reasons:

4.1.1. Improving the Security of Food

Governments and groups can plan for future food shortages or surpluses by using crop prediction to forecast agricultural production in advance. *Crop forecast-based early warning systems can direct operations to control food supplies, maintain reserves, and avert famine.*

4.1.2. Resource Utilization Optimization

Farmers may more effectively distribute labour, water, fertilizer, and pesticides by forecasting crop performance. Agriculture becomes more sustainable as a result of minimizing waste, lowering production costs, and limiting environmental effect.

4.1.3. Reducing Climate Variability Risks

Crop yields are significantly impacted by climate and weather. Climate data is frequently used into crop prediction models to estimate the possible effects of insect outbreaks, floods, and droughts. Farmers can use this information to implement adaptive tactics, such modifying planting schedules or selecting resilient crop varieties.

4.1.4. Aiding with Pricing and Market Planning

By providing traders, exporters, and policymakers with information about anticipated output amounts, accurate crop supply forecasts have an impact on commodities markets. In addition to helping farmers decide when and where to sell their produce, this aids efforts to stabilize prices.

4.1.5. **Enhancing Planning and Agricultural Policy**

Crop forecast data is used by governments to efficiently arrange subsidies, create agricultural policy, and distribute resources. It enhances national agricultural production assessments and makes it possible to more precisely target assistance programs.

4.1.6. **Fostering Innovation in Technology**

Crop prediction promotes the use of cutting-edge technology like AI, machine learning, and remote sensing, which spurs innovation in farming methods and raises overall output.

4.2. Autonomous Tractor: What Is It?

The mainstays of contemporary agriculture have long been tractors. They have been assisting farmers with field ploughs, seeding, and produce transportation since the early 1900s. However, *tractors are gradually becoming more than just mechanical devices; they are becoming intelligent, autonomous machines that can navigate, run, and adjust without the need for human drivers.*

A self-driving agricultural device called an autonomous tractor is made to carry out farming duties without a human operator present. These tractors navigate fields, avoid obstacles, and perform precise tasks like planting, harvesting, and ploughing by utilizing cutting-edge technologies like GPS, sensors, cameras, artificial intelligence (AI), and machine learning algorithms

Autonomous tractors are revolutionizing farming by boosting productivity, decreasing reliance on human labour, and facilitating precision operations, just like self-driving automobiles are modernizing transportation. A *self-driving agricultural vehicle incorporating AI, sensors, GPS, and computer vision technologies* is called an autonomous tractor. It can:

- Detect obstacles and change courses in real time;
- Perform a variety of jobs, including ploughing, tilling, planting, spraying, and harvesting;
- Work constantly, day or night, without human error or tiredness;

While some are semi-autonomous—requiring supervision but handling the majority of tasks on their own—others are completely driverless. Autonomous tractors may run constantly, frequently under remote supervision or control via specialized software, in contrast to standard tractors that need manual control. This increases productivity and lowers labour expenses. They are essential to contemporary precision agriculture, which helps farmers maximize resource utilization, boost output, and lessen human exposure to dangerous or physically taxing field labour.

4.2.1. Diagram: Autonomous (Self-Driving) Tractor

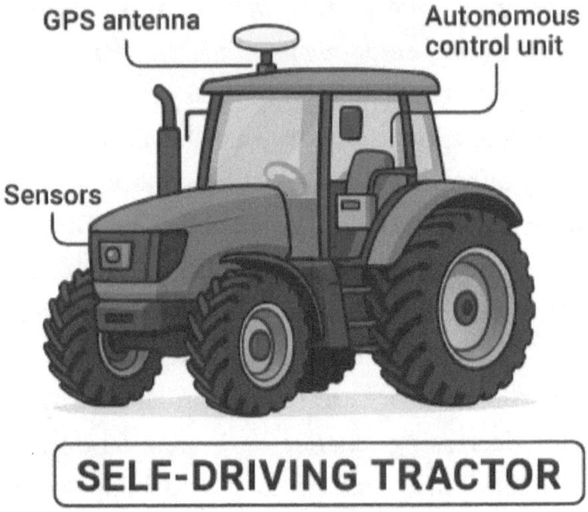

Figure 5: Self-Driving Tractor

4.3. Important Technologies for Self-Driving Tractors

A variety of cutting-edge technologies allow self-driving tractors to function independently, safely, and effectively in a range of agricultural settings. Together, these technologies offer the ability to navigate, make decisions, avoid obstacles, and carry out tasks. Important technologies consist of:

4.3.1. RTK And GPS Navigation

- Autonomous tractors can follow precise paths in the fields thanks to GPS technology, which offers precise location data. For operations like evenly distributing fertilizer or planting seeds at precise intervals, high-precision GPS systems, such *Real-Time Kinematic* (RTK) GPS, guarantee accuracy down to a few centimetres.
- Tractors may follow incredibly exact routes with deviations of less than 2.5 cm when Global Positioning Systems and Real-Time Kinematic (RTK) correction are used together.

4.3.2. Cameras and Sensors

- The tractor uses a variety of sensors to sense its environment, including as LiDAR (Light Detection and Ranging), ultrasonic sensors, radar, and high-resolution cameras.
- These sensors enable the tractor to safely travel and change course as necessary by detecting obstructions, crop rows, terrain features, and other items.

4.3.3. Machine Learning And Artificial Intelligence (AI)

- In order to make judgments in real time, such as avoiding obstacles, planning routes, and modifying operational settings in response to field circumstances, artificial intelligence (AI) algorithms analyse data from sensors and cameras.
- Through learning from prior events and adjusting to changing environments, machine learning allows the tractor to gradually improve its performance.

4.3.4. Remote Monitoring And Telematics

- Through wireless communication networks, telematics systems allow farmers and tractor operators to remotely monitor tractor operations.
- This improves operating effectiveness and safety by enabling remote control, real-time tracking, and diagnostics.

4.3.5. Systems of Autonomous Control

- Without the need for human intervention, sophisticated control systems regulate the tractor's steering, speed, and operation.
- To keep exact control over the tractor's movement and task completion, these systems combine with GPS and sensor data.

4.3.6. Internet of Things (IoT) Integration

- Centralized farm management systems and other smart farming equipment can communicate with autonomous tractors thanks to IoT connectivity.
- Throughout the farm, this connectivity facilitates data sharing, coordinated operations, and efficient resource

management.

4.3.7. Case Study 1: The Autonomous 8R Tractor from John Deere (USA)

John Deere's 8R tractor, which was unveiled in 2022, combines six stereo camera pairs, NVIDIA GPUs for real-time AI processing, and GPS-RTK for autonomous navigation.

Without a human on board, it can negotiate challenging field conditions, plough or till around-the-clock, and provide progress reports to the farmer's mobile app.

Results:

- A 40% increase in operational uptime
- Precise seedbed preparation, increasing yields; • Less reliance on labour during peak season

4.3.8. Case Study 2: Monarch Tractor (USA/India)

With an eye toward both smallholder and industrial farms, **Monarch** created the first fully electric autonomous tractor in history.

Qualities:

- AI-powered self-driving functionality;
- Changeable battery packs;
- Geofencing and collision detection;
- Analytics dashboards and live streaming

Monarch tractors, which are being used by vegetable fields in India and vineyards in California, are simultaneously redefining autonomy and sustainability.

4.3.9. Diagram: Benefits of Autonomous Tractors

Prediction	Action Taken
Labour Efficiency	Lessens the need for qualified drivers, which is crucial given the global labour crisis in agriculture.
Operational Uptime	Able to function consistently even in low-visibility environments
Precision Farming	Depth, spacing, and treatment throughout the field are guaranteed by farming AI.
Cost Savings	Optimized input application, less wear & tear, and decreased fuel consumption
Sustainability	Greenhouse gas emissions are decreased by electric or hybrid models.

Figure 6: Benefits of Autonomous Tractors

4.4. Obstacles and Restrictions

Although autonomous tractors have enormous potential to transform agriculture, their broad use and efficacy are now constrained by a number of issues and limitations. To create solutions that can fully realize their potential, it is imperative to comprehend these difficulties.

4.4.1. **High Initial Cost**

Because they need complex hardware and software, autonomous tractors are far more expensive than conventional tractors. The substantial initial outlay may be unaffordable for farmers with limited resources and small farms.

4.4.2. **Complexity and Maintenance of Technology**

In order to operate, repair, and maintain the sophisticated technologies included in autonomous tractors—such as AI systems, sensors, and GPS—specialized technical knowledge is required. Operational downtime may result from rural locations' limited availability to qualified technicians.

4.4.3. **Limitations of the Infrastructure**

For remote monitoring and management of autonomous tractors, dependable telecommunications infrastructure and internet access are essential. The efficiency of these devices is limited by inadequate network coverage in many rural or undeveloped areas.

4.4.4. **Terrain and Environmental Difficulties**

Obstacles like rocks, uneven ground, or thick vegetation, as well as variable topography and erratic weather patterns, might make it more difficult for the tractor to travel on its own and do duties precisely.

4.4.5. **Safety and Regulatory Issues**

There are legal ambiguities because autonomous farm equipment is not clearly regulated. Furthermore, strong safety procedures and fail-safe mechanisms are necessary to guarantee the security of operators, employees, and spectators around autonomous tractors.

4.4.6. **Risks to Data Security and Privacy**

Large volumes of data are collected and transmitted by autonomous tractors, which raises issues with data protection, cyberattacks, and illegal access. To preserve operational integrity and trust, important agricultural data must be protected.

There are emerging solutions:

- Shared ownership schemes;
- Government funding;
- Kits for modifying current tractors; and
- Mobile control interfaces for customers who are not tech-savvy

4.5. Future Directions for Self-Sustained Agriculture

The goal of self-sustained agriculture is to create farming systems that maximize resource utilization, function well with few outside inputs, and dynamically adjust to changing environmental conditions. This future is being ushered in by autonomous tractors and other innovative technologies. Important instructions consist of:

4.5.1. **Including Autonomous Equipment in Intelligent Farms**

Fleets of networked autonomous tractors and other robotic machinery will cooperate on farms of the future. With the least amount of human involvement, these devices will manage activities like soil preparation, planting, irrigation, pest control, and harvesting, maximizing sustainability and productivity.

4.5.2. **Improved AI and Decision-Making Based on Data**

AI developments will enable self-driving tractors to make wise judgments by analysing real-time data from crop health monitors, soil sensors, and weather forecasts. This entails optimizing yields, cutting waste, and dynamically adapting operations to changes in the environment.

4.5.3. **Electrification and Renewable Energy**

Adoption of electric or hybrid autonomous tractors that run on renewable energy sources like solar or wind will be fuelled by the drive toward sustainability. Over time, this shift will minimize operating costs and greenhouse gas emissions.

4.5.4. **Accurate Resource Administration**

Autonomous tractors combined with precision agriculture technologies will be used by future self-sufficient farms to apply pesticides, fertilizer, and water just where necessary. This focused strategy improves soil health, lessens its negative effects on the environment, and conserves resources.

4.5.5. **Self-Repair and Autonomous Maintenance**

Autonomous tractors may be able to self-diagnose and execute simple maintenance or repairs thanks to emerging technologies, which would reduce downtime and the need for human technicians, particularly in remote areas.

4.5.6. **Support for Policies and Collaborative Environments**

Governments, business leaders, and academic institutions will work together to create infrastructure, standards, and laws that will support the implementation of autonomous agriculture. Programs for farmer training, knowledge exchange, and innovation will be fuelled by public-private partnerships.

4.5.7. **Accessibility and Inclusivity**

The main goal will be to lower the cost and increase the accessibility of autonomous agriculture technologies for smallholder farmers in underdeveloped nations. Expanded involvement in self-sufficient farming systems will be made possible by advancements in modular and scalable technologies.

4.5.8. Case Study 3: Japan's Yanmar Robot Tractor

The **Driverless Tractors** from **Yanmar** fill manpower shortages in elderly rural Japan, where the typical farmer is over 67. A single farmer controls several tractors at once with a tablet using AI-guided technology.

Result:

- A considerable decrease in the amount of time required for rice field preparation during peak season; one farmer can oversee three to four tractors.

4.6. Integrating Precision Agriculture

It takes more than just using cutting-edge equipment to incorporate precision agriculture into farming operations; it involves building a unified, data-driven ecosystem in which all phases of crop production are interconnected for optimal sustainability and efficiency. To provide meaningful information and automate real-time decision-making, this integration entails balancing hardware, software, and human skills.

4.6.1. **Interoperability and Data Consolidation**

Data gathered from a variety of sources, including satellite imaging, drone surveys, Internet of Things sensors, autonomous tractors, and weather stations, is essential to precision agriculture. Interoperable platforms must be used for smooth communication between various systems in order for integration to occur. By combining this data into unified dashboards using AI algorithms, farmers can make well-informed decisions without having to jump between incompatible systems.

4.6.2. **Integrating AI and IoT**

In the Field IoT devices, such climate monitors, nutrient sensors, and soil moisture probes, serve as the farm's sensory organs. These devices, when combined with AI models, are able to detect changes and initiate automated reactions. For instance, they can alter fertilizer application based on real-time nutrient analysis or activate smart irrigation systems when soil moisture falls below ideal levels.

4.6.3. **Connecting Predictive Analytics to Machinery**

To guarantee accurate scheduling of planting, fertilizing, and pest management, predictive AI models can be synced with autonomous tractors, robotic harvesters, and drone sprayers. This enhances crop health, reduces resource waste, and increases production predictability.

4.6.4. **Integration Focused on Farmers**

The effectiveness of a farmer's utilization of technology determines its power. Training programs that enable farmers to understand and accept AI-generated advice, as well as user-friendly interfaces and mobile app accessibility, are all essential components of a successful integration.

4.6.5. **Economic and Environmental Cooperation**

Farms may decrease water waste, optimize energy use, and eliminate chemical misuse by combining all the components of precision agriculture, which will benefit the economy and the environment. This comprehensive integration ensures long-term profitability while promoting climate resilience.

4.6.6. **Important Takeaway:** By converting data into decisions and decisions into sustainable action, precision agriculture integration serves as a link between discrete technical solutions and a completely intelligent farming ecosystem.

4.7. AI in Supply Chain Optimization

The journey from farm to fork encompasses a complex supply chain that includes storage, transportation, processing, distribution, and retail. AI technologies are turning this chain into a lean, transparent, and resilient system that minimizes waste and maximizes value:

4.7.1. **Demand Forecasting**

AI-driven predictive models analyse market trends, seasonal patterns, historical sales data, and even sentiment on social media to accurately forecast demand, allowing producers to match supply with market needs, reducing both surpluses and shortages. 2. Smart Inventory Management Computer vision systems and IoT-enabled storage facilities monitor produce quality in real time, detecting spoilage risks and automatically adjusting storage conditions to prolong shelf life and minimize losses.

4.7.2. **Logistics and Route Optimization**

Logistics platforms driven by AI examine weather forecasts, traffic patterns, and fuel prices to suggest the best routes for transportation, guaranteeing on-time delivery while reducing operating costs.

4.7.3. **Openness and Accountability**

Every stage of a product's journey can be safely documented and validated by fusing blockchain technology with artificial intelligence. In addition to enhancing consumer confidence, this aids in identifying the sources of contamination in food safety events.

4.7.4. **Optimization of Prices**

In order to recommend dynamic pricing strategies that enable farmers and suppliers to maintain their competitiveness without compromising profitability, machine learning algorithms continuously assess market conditions.

4.7.5. **Reducing Waste by Redistribution**

Artificial intelligence (AI) systems can identify excess product early and link it to food banks, processors, or secondary marketplaces, reducing needless waste.

4.7.6. **Key Takeaway:** AI supply chain·optimization ensures that agricultural benefits are converted into sustained earnings and less waste by bridging the gap between farm output and consumer demand.

Chapter 5: Intelligent Irrigation Systems: Water is Wisdom

5.1. Water Is the Most Valuable Resource in Agriculture

More than *70% of the freshwater used in agriculture is wasted because of excessive irrigation, poor timing, and antiquated infrastructure.* Drought, climate change, and groundwater depletion are posing serious problems for food production in many areas.

Farmers' water management practices are being revolutionized by smart irrigation systems driven by *Internet of Things* (IoT) and *Artificial Intelligence* (AI) technologies. These technologies guarantee that crops receive precisely the right amount of water—neither more nor less—at the right time and in the most effective manner.

5.2. Smart Irrigation: What Is It?

The automation and optimization of watering schedules and volumes using *Artificial Intelligence* (AI) and real-time environmental data is known as *Smart Irrigation*. Smart systems adjust to dynamic variables such soil moisture, weather forecasts, crop growth stage, *Evapotranspiration* (ET) rates, and water availability, in contrast to traditional irrigation, which adheres to set routines.

Using information from sensors, weather forecasts, soil moisture levels, crop growth phases, and historical trends, intelligent watering is an AI-driven irrigation technique that provides the appropriate amount of water at the appropriate time and location. Intelligent watering systems continuously assess current circumstances and automatically modify irrigation to maximize plant health and resource efficiency, in contrast to conventional watering techniques that depend on set schedules or human monitoring.

Fundamentally, intelligent watering incorporates:

- Internet of Things sensors to measure temperature, humidity, and soil moisture.
- AI algorithms that forecast future water requirements based on weather forecasts, crop models, and evapotranspiration rates; • Satellite and drone imagery to evaluate crop health and identify water stress zones.
- Automated control systems that precisely administer water where it is needed, including smart pumps and valves.

Among the advantages are:

- **Water conservation**, which minimizes waste and prevents excessive irrigation.

- **Higher crop yields** because the soil is kept at the ideal moisture content for every stage of growth.
- **Lower expenses** – less energy is used for labour-intensive operations and pumps.
- **Climate resilience** - modifying irrigation plans in response to shifting meteorological conditions.

Essentially, intelligent watering helps farmers increase output while protecting water resources by converting irrigation from a guesswork-based process to a data-driven precision practice.

5.3. Important Elements of Intelligent Irrigation Systems

In order to monitor, evaluate, and regulate water distribution in real time, intelligent watering uses a variety of state-of-the-art technology. In irrigation systems, these technologies guarantee accuracy, effectiveness, and flexibility.

5.3.1. **Internet of Things-Based Environmental and Soil Sensors**

- Take measurements of the temperature, humidity, nutrient levels, and soil moisture at various depths.
- Offer ongoing, site-specific data to help guide irrigation choices.

5.3.2. **Algorithms for Decision-Making Driven by AI**

- To ascertain the precise water requirements for every agricultural zone, examine sensor data, crop models, and weather forecasts.
- Forecast future water needs by using seasonal patterns and plant growth stages.

5.3.3. **Imaging and Remote Sensing**

- Broad trends in water stress across fields can be found using satellite images.
- Early indicators of crop stress and local moisture fluctuations are detected by drone-based multispectral imagery.

5.3.4. **Smart Irrigation Controllers:**

- These are automated systems that use AI recommendations to operate or close irrigation pumps and valves.
- Use weather data to minimize output during cooler weather or to forego watering when it rains.

5.3.5. **Platforms for Cloud-Based Data**

- For analysis, reporting, and long-term trend tracking, centralize all irrigation data.
- Give farmers the ability to remotely modify irrigation using dashboards or mobile apps.

5.3.6. **Weather Forecast Integration:**

- Predicts rainfall, temperature changes, and evaporation rates using hyperlocal weather data.
- Optimizes water efficiency and avoids overwatering.

5.3.7. **Systems of Variable Rate Irrigation (VRI)**

- Permit varying fields to get varying quantities of water according on slope, crop health, and soil type.
- Assure optimal yield and consistent crop growth.

5.3.8. **Diagram: How AI Enhances Irrigation**

AI improves irrigation in a number of significant ways:

Function	AI Application
Scheduling	Uses predictive models to determine the optimal time of day and frequency of irrigation.
Zonal Watering	Applies varying quantities to various zones according to crop and soil data.
Evapotranspiration Modelling	Estimates daily water loss and plans replacement using weather and crop data.
Leakage Detection	Uses pattern recognition to find irregularities in the flow of water.
Autonomous Operation	Automatically starts irrigation when predetermined moisture thresholds are reached.

Figure 7: How AI Enhances Irrigation

5.4. Benefits of Smart Watering

Beyond conventional irrigation, intelligent watering offers revolutionary benefits for contemporary agriculture, resulting in a more intelligent and sustainable farming system:

5.4.1. **Water Conservation:**

- This minimizes waste by only providing the water that plants truly require.
- Prevents overwatering, which can lead to soil erosion and nutrient leakage.

5.4.2. **Higher Yields from Crops**

- Preserves ideal soil moisture levels during the plant growth cycle.
- Lessens plant stress, resulting in better harvests and healthier crops.

5.4.3. **Cost Savings:**

- By cutting down on pump run times, energy consumption is decreased.
- Reduces labour costs by using remote control and automation.

5.4.4. **Resilience to Climate Change**

- Instantaneously adjusts to shifting weather conditions.
- Assists farmers in managing severe heat events, erratic rainfall, and droughts.

5.4.5. **Environmental Protection:**

- Prevents excessive irrigation from contaminating groundwater and runoff.
- Saves water supplies for coming generations.

5.4.6. **Precision Farming Integration:**

- This technology integrates easily with other smart farming technologies, such as variable rate fertilization and AI-based crop monitoring.
- Boosts the general effectiveness of agricultural management.

5.4.7. **Information-Based Perspectives**

- Produces real-time and historical data to improve long-term planning.
- Aids in forecasting future watering requirements through predictive modelling.

5.4.8. Case Study 1: Israel's AI Drip Irrigation System from Netafim

AI powers **Precision Irrigation-as-a-Service** from Netafim, a leader in drip irrigation. Their methods use data from satellites and soil sensors; AI models to forecast agricultural water consumption; and automated drip line control.

Results:

- Up to 40% less water was used.
- A 30% improvement in yield
- Significant decreases in fertilizer runoff

Every drop matters in sustainable farming made possible by Netafim, which is extensively used in water-scarce areas like Chile, South Africa, and India.

5.4.9. Case Study 2: CropX (USA/New Zealand)

CropX combines meteorological, crop stage, and topographic data with AI to assess soil moisture data from wireless probes.

Important Features Include:

- Recommendations for irrigation based on apps
- AI notifications for excessive or insufficient irrigation;
- Integration with current irrigation machinery
- During dry conditions, farmers report increased crop stability and input savings of up to 25%.

5.5. Smart Irrigation Techniques for Smallholder Farmers

Large farms aren't the only ones using AI irrigation.

Start-ups such as:

- **KhethWorks (India)** provide vegetable producers with inexpensive irrigation pumps that are AI-scheduled.
- **iRain (Africa)** uses satellite rainfall prediction models to send smallholders SMS-based irrigation advisories.
- **Sencrop (Europe)** provides reasonably priced AI weather-driven irrigation systems to help fruit and grain growers prevent frost and drought damage.

These platforms democratise AI access through:

- Solar-powered sensor;
- Mobile phones
- Services that are subscription-based.

5.5.1. Diagram: Advantages of Smart Irrigation

Benefits	Impact
Water Efficiency	Using up to 50% less water while preserving or boosting yield.
Reduced Costs	Reduced water and energy costs.
Soil Health	Reduces the danger of salinization and waterlogging.
Labour Savings	Automation decreases the need for manual switching and monitoring.
Crop Health Quality	Higher market value and improved crop quality are the results of uniform irrigation.
Environmental Protection	Fertilizer leaching is reduced, and pumping system emissions are decreased.

Figure 8: Advantages of Smart Irrigation

5.6. Integrating with Crop and Weather Models

AI-driven irrigation can interface with:

- Weather APIs, such as OpenWeather and IBM's Weather Company.
- Crop growth models, such as DSSAT and AquaCrop
- **Field Digital Twins:** Models that are simulated to test irrigation techniques in a virtual environment before being implemented

This makes it possible to manage water in a hyper-localized, forward-looking manner even during erratic weather conditions.

5.7. Smart Irrigation's Drawbacks and Restrictions

Although there are many benefits to smart irrigation, farmers and other stakeholders must overcome certain operational, financial, and technical obstacles before it can be widely used.

5.7.1. **Expensive Upfront Expenses**

- The initial outlay for automated controllers, AI systems, and smart sensors is high.
- Without subsidies or funding, small-scale farmers could find it impossible to pay for installation.

5.7.2. **Technical Complexity**:

- Installing, configuring, and maintaining the system calls for certain knowledge.
- To understand data and follow AI recommendations, farmers might require training.

5.7.3. **Reliance On Connectivity To The Internet**

- Reliable internet connectivity is frequently required for cloud-based platforms and real-time monitoring, but it may be scarce in rural locations.
- In certain areas, offline-capable solutions are still lacking.

5.7.4. **Requirements for Power Supplies**

- The energy or solar power used by automated pumps, controls, and sensors is not always reliable.
- Schedules for watering may be disrupted by power

interruptions.

5.7.5. **Maintenance and Calibration of Sensors**

- To guarantee accuracy, sensors need to be routinely inspected and calibrated.
- Over time, harsh environmental conditions can harm equipment.

5.7.6. **Data Security and Privacy Issues**

- Keeping farm and irrigation data on the cloud raises possible cybersecurity issues.
- Farmers require reassurance that private data won't be abused.

5.7.7. **Integration Difficulties**

- Intelligent watering systems need to integrate easily with other precision farming technology and the current irrigation infrastructure.
- With older equipment, compatibility problems may occur.

5.7.8. **ROI Uncertainty:** Depending on the crop variety, climate, and market conditions, it may take multiple growing seasons for the financial return on investment to become apparent.

5.8. Smart Irrigation's Future Directions

More automation, deeper AI integration, and more accessibility for farmers of all sizes are key components of the future of smart irrigation. Smart irrigation systems will change from being a high-end solution to a common agricultural necessity as technology advances.

1. **AI-Driven Predictive Irrigation**:

- Using machine learning models, future systems will predict water requirements days or weeks in advance.
- Crop genetics, past yield trends, and seasonal climatic trends will all be taken into account in the predictions.

    1. **Self-Learning Irrigation Networks:**

- By learning from previous performance, systems will automatically adjust over time.
- Without human assistance, algorithms will adjust water delivery to maximize yield and resource efficiency.

    1. **Advanced Sensor Miniaturization**:

- Small-scale farms will find it easier to adopt sensors that are smaller, less expensive, and more energy-efficient.
- For incredibly accurate moisture monitoring, nano-sensors can be affixed to plant roots or placed straight into the soil.

    1. **Integration with Autonomous Machinery:**

- To create a completely automated crop management cycle, intelligent watering will be connected to drones, robotic planters, and self-driving tractors.

- Within minutes of identification, irrigation drones may provide tailored water to places under stress.

1. **Blockchain for Transparency in Water Data**

- Blockchain technology may monitor and confirm water use, guaranteeing adherence to sustainability guidelines.
- This will help farms receive water conservation credits and eco-certifications.

1. **Irrigation Powered by Renewable Energy**

- The use of hybrid, solar, and wind energy will lessen dependency on the grid.
- Intelligent irrigation systems that are completely off the grid will become practical, especially in isolated areas.

1. **Democratization of Access**:

- In poor nations, low-cost intelligent watering kits will be created for smallholder farmers.
- In order to guarantee food security and water sustainability, governments and non-governmental organizations will progressively fund adoption.

1. **Models Adaptive to Climate Change**

- AI algorithms will adapt irrigation for droughts, floods, and changing rainfall patterns by taking into account real-time climate change indicators.
- Because of this, climate-resilient agriculture will rely heavily on intelligent irrigation.

5.9. AI-Driven Smart Irrigation Systems

The next step in agricultural water management is represented by AI-powered smart irrigation systems, which combine cutting-edge artificial intelligence with real-time environmental monitoring to guarantee crop irrigation that is sustainable, accurate, and efficient. These systems, in contrast to traditional irrigation, constantly modify water distribution in response to data-driven insights, guaranteeing ideal plant growth while preserving resources.

1. **Fundamental Idea**

AI is used by smart irrigation systems to:

- Gather information from weather stations, drones, satellites, and soil moisture sensors.
- Examine the data to determine the water requirements of the crops.
- Take action by setting irrigation equipment to automatically provide the appropriate amount of water at the appropriate time.

1. **Essential Elements**

- **Real-Time Monitoring:** Constant observation of plant health, soil moisture, and microclimate variables.
- **Adaptive Water Scheduling:** AI systems modify watering plans according on crop type, stage of growth, and environmental factors.
- **Predictive Analytics:** This method forecasts future irrigation requirements by examining past trends, evapotranspiration rates, and weather forecasts.

- **Remote Management**: Using online dashboards, tablets, or cellphones, farmers can keep an eye on and manage irrigation.

1. **Advantages**

- **Water Savings:** Accurate application reduces waste.
- **Increased Yields:** Preserves the optimal conditions for crop growth.
- **Lower Costs:** This lowers the labour and energy costs related to manual irrigation.
- **Environmental Protection**: Reduces nutrient leaching and runoff.

1. **AI Application Examples**

- Machine learning models that use images to identify early indicators of agricultural water stress.
- Neural networks that simultaneously optimize the timing of irrigation for several crops.
- Computer vision systems that use drones to track soil cracks and leaf withering.

1. **Connectivity to Wider Farm Systems**

The following are the best connections for smart irrigation:

- Precision Agriculture Platforms for integrated soil and crop management.
- Fertilizer delivery systems that integrate fertigation, or the application of nutrients and irrigation.
- Adapting to changing weather patterns using climate-resilient farming techniques.

5.2.1. Elements of Smart Irrigation Systems Driven by AI

Hardware, software, and connectivity tools form the foundation of AI-powered smart irrigation systems, which monitor, analyse, and regulate water delivery. Every element is essential to maintaining accuracy, effectiveness, and flexibility:

5.2.1. Sensor Network

- **Soil Moisture Sensors:** To guarantee that roots get the right amount of moisture, these sensors measure the water content at different depths.
- **Environmental Sensors**: Monitor rainfall, wind speed, temperature, and humidity.
- **Nutrient Sensors:** Keep an eye on the levels of nutrients in the soil to combine fertilization and watering.

5.2.2. **Data Processing Unit (On-Farm Or Cloud-Based)**

- Unit that gathers unprocessed sensor data and sends it to artificial intelligence models.
- It can be transmitted to cloud platforms for sophisticated analytics or included in edge computing devices for local decision-making.

5.2.3. **Machine Learning Models and AI Algorithms**

- Examine trends in weather, crop health, and water use.
- Forecast future watering requirements and identify irregularities like leaks or sensor mistakes.

5.2.4. **Remote Sensing Tools**

- **Satellite Imagery:** Offers extensive tracking of water distribution and vegetation health.
- Multispectral camera-equipped drones may locate tense

areas in a field that require focused irrigation.

5.2.5. **Hardware for Irrigation Control**

- AI-recommended opening and closing of automated pumps and valves.
- **Variable Rate Irrigation (VRI) Systems**: These systems use varying quantities of water in various field zones.
- Integrated drip, sprinkler, or pivot systems for accurate delivery.

5.2.6. **Infrastructure for Connectivity**

- **Wireless Networks**, such as 5G, NB-IoT, and LoRa, guarantee dependable data transfer between devices.
- **Gateway Devices:** Serve as links between sensors and the cloud or internet.

5.2.7. **Management Dashboard and User Interface**

- Reachable by PCs, tablets, or smartphones.
- Provides farmers with real-time data, analytics, alerts, and control options.
- **Power Supply:** Off-grid, sustainable power for rural deployments is provided by solar panels.
- **Battery Backup:** This guarantees continuous operation in the event of an outage.

5.3. How AI Increases the Effectiveness of Irrigation

By maximizing water consumption, reducing waste, and enhancing crop health through intelligent data analysis and automated control, artificial intelligence improves irrigation efficiency. This is how AI contributes:

5.3.1. **Precision Watering**:

- AI analyses information from several sources, including plant conditions, soil moisture, and weather predictions, to provide water precisely where and when it is required.
- This lessens under-irrigation, which stresses plants, and over-irrigation, which can result in runoff and nutrient loss.

5.3.2. **Dynamic Scheduling:**

- AI automatically modifies irrigation timing and quantities in response to real-time environmental changes, replacing predefined watering schedules.
- For instance, during heat waves, irrigation may be increased or skipped before rainfall.

5.3.3. **Early Stress Detection**:

- By analysing sensor and picture data, machine learning algorithms are able to identify early indicators of disease or drought stress, enabling focused interventions before damage is apparent.

5.3.4. **Resource Optimization**

- AI reduces energy usage and equipment wear and tear by optimizing pump operation.
- In order to accommodate different soil types and crop requirements, it also facilitates variable rate irrigation, which applies water differently across field zones.

5.3.5. **Predictive Maintenance:**

- AI keeps an eye on system performance to spot leaks, obstructions, or sensor issues, allowing for prompt repairs and averting flooding.

5.3.6. **Integration with Other Farm Data**

- AI develops a comprehensive management plan that optimizes whole farm productivity by merging irrigation data with information on fertilization, pest control, and yield.

5.3.7. **Learning and Adaptation**

- AI systems get better over time by continuously improving their algorithms for increased accuracy and efficiency by learning from previous irrigation results.

5.4. Practical Illustrations of AI-Powered Smart Irrigation

AI-powered smart irrigation systems have been successfully deployed by a number of farms and agricultural businesses globally, indicating their potential to completely transform agricultural water management. Here are a few noteworthy instances:

5.4.1. **John Deere's Precision Irrigation Technology:**

- Automates irrigation decisions for large farms by combining meteorological data, soil sensors, and AI analytics.
- Customizes water application using variable rate irrigation, which significantly reduces water use and increases yield.

5.4.2. **CropX Soil Sensor Platform:**

- This platform gives farmers access to a cloud-based dashboard that analyses soil texture and moisture data using artificial intelligence.
- Uses simple-to-install sensors to improve water use by providing irrigation suggestions specific to field zones.

5.4.3. **Prospera Technologies**

- Uses AI-powered image analysis from fixed cameras and drones to track crop health and identify water stress early.
- Provides real-time reaction and increased water efficiency by connecting insights to automated irrigation systems.

5.4.4. **Rachio Smart Sprinkler Controller:**

- This consumer-grade smart irrigation controller optimizes lawn watering schedules by utilizing AI and weather forecasts.
- It demonstrates how AI may improve irrigation's efficiency and usability, but mostly for household use.

5.4.5. **Jain Irrigation Systems**:

- Combines sensor data with AI to lower water use while maintaining high agricultural yields, particularly in water-scarce locations; uses IoT and AI in drip irrigation settings across commercial farms in India.

5.4.6. **Taranis Agricultural Intelligence:**

- This system uses AI algorithms and multispectral drone imagery to identify water stress and trigger irrigation alarms automatically.
- Makes proactive irrigation management possible, which lowers water consumption and increases output.

5.5. Difficulties in Implementing AI-Powered Smart Irrigation

Despite the revolutionary potential of AI-powered smart irrigation, a number of obstacles stand in the way of its successful implementation and broad adoption:

5.5.1. **High Initial Cost**

- For small and medium-sized farms, the price of sensors, AI software, and automated watering equipment may be too high.
- In underdeveloped nations, access is restricted by a lack of reasonably priced funding or subsidies.

5.5.2. **Technical Know-How and Training**

- To comprehend, use, and maintain AI-based systems, farmers might need training.
- Inadequate local technical assistance may make a system less effective.

5.5.3. **Limitations of the Infrastructure**

- Rural farming locations frequently lack dependable power supplies and internet connectivity, which might interfere with automated controls and data transfer.

5.5.4. **Data Management and Privacy**

- Farmers may worry about the ownership and privacy of their agricultural data, and managing massive amounts of sensor and satellite data calls for secure cloud infrastructure.

5.5.5. **System Integration:**

- It might be challenging to integrate AI irrigation solutions with other farm management systems and current irrigation infrastructure.
- Compatibility problems can necessitate further expenditures or improvements.

5.5.6. **Variability in the Environment**

- The accuracy of AI predictions may be hampered by unknown soil conditions, extreme weather, or abrupt weather changes.
- Systems need to be resilient and flexible in the face of such fluctuations.

5.5.7. **Upkeep and Sensor Dependability**

- Due to their exposure to harsh agricultural settings, sensors and devices may need to be calibrated or replaced on a regular basis.
- Inaccurate irrigation decisions may result from malfunctioning sensors.

5.6. Upcoming Developments in AI-Powered Smart Irrigation

With new technology and creative ideas, the development of AI-powered smart irrigation is set to pick up speed, making irrigation even more accurate, effective, and widely available. Important upcoming trends consist of:

5.6.1. On-Device Processing and Edge AI:

- By bringing AI computations closer to the sensors (on the edge), reliance on cloud connectivity will be lessened, enabling real-time decision-making even in offline or low-internet conditions.

5.6.2. **Combining Autonomous Systems and Robotics**

- Autonomous farm equipment like robotic sprayers and irrigation drones will increasingly be integrated with smart irrigation; these systems may precisely apply water where AI identifies stress, allowing for large-scale, targeted treatments.

5.6.3. **Enhanced Multisensory Fusion:**

- This comprehensive sensing strategy will better capture climatic fluctuations and crop needs by combining data from many sensor types, including soil, weather, plant physiology, satellite, and drone imaging. It will also increase AI accuracy.

5.6.4. **AI-Driven Water Rights and Usage Tracking:**

- Blockchain technology and artificial intelligence will make it possible to trace water usage transparently and impenetrably, promoting sustainable water management and regulatory compliance.

5.6.5. **Scalable and Inexpensive Smallholder Solutions**

- The creation of open-source AI platforms and inexpensive sensors will democratize access for small and resource-poor farmers, and governments and non-governmental organizations will be essential in funding and expanding these technologies.

5.6.6. **Climate-Adaptive Irrigation Models:**

- In order to help farmers react to changing weather patterns, AI models will increasingly take climate change projections into account when adjusting irrigation tactics.

5.6.7. **Decision Support Systems Driven by AI**

- Future systems will offer integrated guidance on fertilization, pest control, and harvest time in addition to irrigation control.
- As a result, smart irrigation will be a component of an ecosystem for digital farm management.

5.7. Self-sufficient Irrigation Equipment

By fusing robots, artificial intelligence, and precision irrigation technology, autonomous irrigation equipment advances agricultural automation by automating water distribution with little assistance from humans. These systems allow for accurate watering that is adapted to crop requirements and field circumstances, while also increasing efficiency and lowering labour expenses.

5.7.1. Autonomous Irrigation Machines: What Are They?

Self-operating devices that travel fields on their own and modify water application depending on real-time data are outfitted with sensors, GPS, artificial intelligence, and actuators to do irrigation operations automatically.

5.7.2. Autonomous Irrigation Equipment Types

- **Autonomous Irrigation Drones**: Frequently utilized in vineyards and orchards, these drones fly across fields to precisely spray water where needed.
- **Self-Driving Irrigation Tractors**: With pivot or drip irrigation systems installed, self-driving irrigation tractors traverse fields in accordance with AI-guided patterns.
- **Robotic Irrigation Units:** These are ground robots that move across crops and use drip lines or precision nozzles to provide water.

5.7.3. Fundamental Technologies

- Accurate navigation and irrigation zone mapping are made possible by **GPS and GIS mapping**.
- **Machine Learning:** Using information on soil, crop health, and weather, machine learning optimizes irrigation

schedules.

- **Sensors:** Real-time detection of environmental factors, plant stress, and soil moisture.
- **Automated Actuators:** These devices precisely manage water flow by controlling pumps, valves, and spray nozzles.

5.7.4. Advantages

- Lowers operating expenses and human labour.
- Improves the efficiency and regularity of watering.
- Makes irrigation possible in dangerous or challenging terrain.
- Offers information for ongoing system enhancement.

5.7.5. Difficulties

- Expensive initial outlays and complicated technology.
- It can be difficult to integrate with the current irrigation infrastructure; it requires strong maintenance and expert operation.

5.8. Essential Elements of Self-Driving Irrigation Equipment

To function successfully and efficiently in the field, autonomous irrigation equipment combines a number of cutting-edge technology and parts. Gaining an understanding of these elements is crucial to understanding the operation of these devices and their significance in contemporary agriculture.

5.8.1. Systems for Positioning and Navigation

- **Receivers for GNSS and GPS:** To traverse fields and adhere to irrigation courses that have been pre-programmed, provide accurate location tracking.
- **Inertial Measurement Units (IMUs):** Provide movement detection and orientation support for precise manoeuvring.
- **GIS Mapping Software**: aids in the development of water distribution routes and irrigation zones.

5.8.2. Arrays Of Sensors

- **Soil Moisture Sensors:** Track water content to inform real-time irrigation choices.
- **Environmental Sensors**: Monitor solar radiation, wind speed, temperature, and humidity to modify watering schedules.
- **Plant Health Sensors:** To evaluate crop stress, use spectral imaging or NDVI (Normalized Difference Vegetation Index) sensors.

5.8.3. Control Systems and AI

- **AI Processors On Board:** evaluate sensor data, decide how to water, and operate machinery on their own.

- **Machine Learning Algorithms**: By using field conditions and previous data, these algorithms continuously increase irrigation efficiency.
- **Obstacle Detection and Avoidance:** To safely avoid obstacles, use LIDAR, ultrasonic, or camera sensors.

5.8.4. Mechanisms for Delivering Water

- **Variable Rate Irrigation (VRI) Systems:** Provide exact control over the amount of water supplied to various field segments.
- Depending on the crop and topography, sprayers, drip lines, or spray nozzles are designed to apply water efficiently.
- Pump and valve controls are automated parts that manage the pressure and flow of water.

5.8.5. Power Systems

- **Battery Packs or Hybrid Systems:** These supply energy for self-sufficient functioning and are frequently paired with solar panels for environmental sustainability.
- **Energy Management Modules**: Increase operating time by optimizing power use.

5.8.6. Communication Interfaces

- **Wireless Connectivity (Wi-Fi, LTE, 5G, LoRa):** Makes it possible to send data to farm management systems and monitor and control them remotely.
- **User Interfaces**: Dashboards and mobile apps that let farmers monitor and modify operations from a distance.

5.9. Benefits and Drawbacks of Self-Driving Irrigation Equipment

Although autonomous irrigation equipment has several advantages for contemporary farming, there are some issues that must be resolved for best use.

5.9.1. Benefits

1. **Labour Savings:** By eliminating the need for human labour in irrigation activities, this solution addresses labour shortages and lowers operating expenses.
2. **Precision Watering**: This technique enhances crop health and water use efficiency by precisely applying water based on real-time data.
3. **Consistent Operation:** Regardless of human availability, this system runs around-the-clock in accordance with pre-set instructions, guaranteeing timely irrigation.
4. **Access to Difficult Terrain**: Identifies regions, including steep slopes or uneven fields that can be dangerous or difficult for manual watering.
5. **Data Collection and Analytics:** Field data is continuously gathered and analysed to improve irrigation and farm management in general.
6. **Integration Potential:** For comprehensive precision agriculture, it can be combined with other self-governing equipment and farm management systems.

5.9.2. **Restrictions**

1. **High Initial Investment:** Large upfront expenses may be prohibitive, particularly for smallholder farmers or farms located in underdeveloped nations.

2. **Technical Complexity:** May restrict accessibility due to the need for technical know-how for operation, maintenance, and troubleshooting.
3. **Dependency on Power and Connectivity:** Operations may be disrupted by power outages or inadequate coverage; this depends on dependable energy sources and network connectivity.
4. **Maintenance Requirements:** To operate at their best, mechanical components and sensitive sensors need to be calibrated and maintained on a regular basis.
5. **Integration Challenges**: When integrating with other farm systems or modifying existing irrigation infrastructure, compatibility problems could occur.
6. **Environmental Constraints:** Unexpected impediments, variable soil, and extreme weather can all have an impact on machine dependability and performance.

5.10. New Developments in Self-Driving Irrigation Equipment

Autonomous irrigation equipment is developing quickly as technology progresses. These new developments suggest more accessible, adaptable, and intelligent solutions that will further revolutionize agricultural water management.

5.10.1. Swarm Robotics:

- A group of tiny, self-sufficient irrigation robots that cooperate to effectively cover big fields.
- Makes scaling irrigation possible with flexibility and redundancy.

5.10.2. AI-Powered Decision-Making and Navigation

- Real-time crop, soil, and obstacle recognition is improved through the use of deep learning and computer vision.
- Enhances accuracy and security when operating autonomously.

5.10.3. Hybrid Energy Solutions

- Off-grid farms can benefit from energy-autonomous irrigation equipment that combines solar, wind, and battery storage.
- Lowers operating expenses and the carbon footprint.

5.10.4. Adaptive and Modular Designs

- Devices with detachable irrigation modules (such as misting, sprinkler, and drip) that are adapted to the type of crop and stage of growth.

- Does not require separate machinery to meet a variety of agriculture demands.

5.10.5. Connectivity to Big Data and IoT Platforms

- Data is fed into farm-wide management systems via autonomous machines, allowing for centralized decision-making.
- Facilitates comprehensive optimization for harvesting, pest management, fertilization, and irrigation.

5.10.6. Improved Remote Control and User Interfaces

- Enhanced mobile applications and augmented reality (AR) interfaces for remote machinery monitoring, control, and troubleshooting.
- Reduces technical obstacles for technicians and farmers.

5.10.7. Safety and Regulatory Improvements

- The creation of certificates and standards to guarantee that self-sufficient irrigation equipment conforms with environmental and safety requirements.
- Encourages greater user trust and acceptance.

5.11. AI in Agriculture's Water Resource Management

Sustainable agriculture depends on efficient management of water resources, particularly in light of climate change, water shortage, and rising food demand. In order to guarantee long-term availability and efficiency, AI is essential to improving water use at the agricultural, regional, and watershed levels.

5.11.1. An Overview of AI in the Management of Water Resources

- AI systems help decision-making for effective water distribution and conservation by analysing large datasets, including hydrological models, weather patterns, soil moisture, and crop water requirements.

5.11.2. AI Applications for Water Management in Agriculture

- **Irrigation Scheduling Optimization**: AI determines ideal timing and quantity for irrigation to increase agricultural output and decrease water use.
- **Water Allocation and Distribution**: Predictive models help ensure that farmers and regions receive an equitable share of the scarce water resources.
- **Drought Monitoring and Early Warning:** AI forecasts droughts and initiates mitigation strategies by analysing climatic data.
- **Leak and Loss Detection**: AI and sensors work together to find irrigation network leaks and stop water loss.
- **Rainwater Harvesting Optimization**: To augment irrigation requirements, AI plans and controls rainwater

collection systems.

5.11.3. **Advantages**

- Enhances water use efficiency at both micro (farm) and macro (watershed) scales.
- Supports sustainable water practices lowering environmental effect.
- Increases resistance to climatic extremes and fluctuation.

5.11.4. **Difficulties**

- The quality and accessibility of data at the regional level.
- Including AI findings in frameworks for water governance and policy.
- Ensuring that all stakeholders have fair access to AI-driven water management solutions.

5.12. AI Methods Used in the Management of Agricultural Water Resources

AI uses a range of methods to evaluate intricate water data and maximize management plans in a range of agricultural environments. Important AI strategies include:

5.12.1. Machine Learning (ML)

- **Supervised Learning:** Using past weather and soil data, models are trained on labelled datasets to forecast water demand, drought risk, or irrigation requirements.

- **Unsupervised Learning**: This method, which may be used to identify leaks or group related water demand zones, finds patterns and abnormalities in sensor data or water usage without the need for established labels.

5.12.2. Deep Learning:

- This technique improves prediction accuracy and spatial precision by processing massive and diverse datasets, such as sensor networks, satellite imagery, and climate models, using multi-layer neural networks.

5.12.3. Reinforcement Learning:

- This technique improves irrigation scheduling and resource distribution dynamically by modelling the best water allocation strategies based on environmental feedback.

5.12.4. Predictive Analytics:

- This technique uses time-series analysis and climate data integration to forecast future drought events, crop water requirements, and water availability.

5.12.5. Remote Sensing and Computer Vision

- Analyses drone and satellite imagery to evaluate water bodies, vegetation health, and soil moisture, supplying data for artificial intelligence models.

5.12.6. Optimization Algorithms:

- Optimize water efficiency under restrictions such as limited supply or conflicting demands by resolving intricate scheduling and allocation issues.

5.12.7. Integration of the Internet of Things (IoT):

- This integrates AI with sensor networks to provide automated response and real-time water monitoring in irrigation and water distribution systems.

5.13. AI Case Studies for Agricultural Water Resource Management

Global agriculture is changing as a result of AI's use in water resource management. Here are some noteworthy instances illustrating its influence:

5.13.1. Israel's AI-Driven Water Management:

In water-scarce regions, Israel optimizes irrigation schedules using AI models combined with vast sensor networks and satellite data. The technology increases water use efficiency by up to 40%, allowing for sustainable farming even with restricted water supplies.

5.13.2. California's Drought Prediction and Water Allocation System: To forecast drought conditions and optimize water distribution among farmers and urban users, California uses machine learning algorithms. These predictive models assist farmers and policymakers in making well-informed decisions, thereby reducing the effects of drought.

5.13.3. The Smart Water Grid Project in India uses mobile platforms, IoT sensors, and AI analytics to track water demand and supply in agricultural areas. Demand forecasting and leak detection powered by AI lower water losses and increase farmers' supply stability.

5.13.4. Murray-Darling Basin Water Management in Australia: The basin's water distribution is managed using AI and big data analytics to strike a balance between ecological protection and agricultural demands. During periods of severe drought, adaptive water management is supported by real-time data monitoring and predictive models.

5.13.5. Smart Irrigation Pilot in Spain: This project optimized irrigation in vineyards by combining AI, IoT sensors, and remote sensing; the results indicated a 25% reduction in water usage without compromising crop quality or output.

5.14. AI-Based Water Resource Management:

5.14.1. Challenges and Prospects

Water resource management powered by AI has the potential to be revolutionary, but it also faces a number of challenges and exciting opportunities.

5.14.2. Challenges

1. **Availability and Quality of Data**: High-resolution, dependable data is crucial but frequently scarce, particularly in poor nations; inconsistent or missing data can lower the efficacy and accuracy of models.

2. **Infrastructure Restrictions:** It can be expensive and logistically challenging to deploy and maintain IoT sensors over vast, frequently isolated agricultural regions.

3. **Integration with Governance and Policy**: Technologists, legislators, and farmers must work together to translate AI discoveries into practical water management regulations; regulatory frameworks may not keep up with technology advancements.

4. **Equity and Access:** Farmers who are smallholders or marginalized may not have access to AI technologies and associated infrastructure, which could lead to a widening of gaps.

5. **Complexity of Water Systems**:

Modelling and prediction are difficult due to the many factors that influence agricultural water systems, such as hydrology, climate, and socioeconomics.

5.14.3. Prospects

1. **Increased Sustainability**: AI makes it possible to use water more efficiently, which helps to save limited supplies and lessen environmental effects.
2. **Increased Resilience**: Adaptive management and early warning systems increase readiness for floods, droughts, and climatic variability.
3. **Cost Efficiency:** By automating monitoring and decision-making procedures, AI can lower operating expenses.
4. **Data-Driven Policy Making:** Evidence-based resource allocation and water governance are supported by improved data analytics.
5. **Inclusive Technology Deployment** AI can be modified for smallholder farmers with focused assistance, fostering fair access and advantages.

5.15. Overview and Prospects for Artificial Intelligence in Agricultural Water Management

The management of agricultural water resources is fast changing due to artificial intelligence, which is propelling a change toward sustainability, efficiency, and precision. AI makes data-driven decisions that save water, increase crop yields, and strengthen resistance to climate variability possible in everything from smart irrigation equipment and watering systems to large-scale water resource distribution.

Key Takeaways:

- AI optimizes irrigation at the farm and regional levels by integrating a variety of data sources, including satellite imaging, weather forecasts, and soil sensors.
- AI-powered control systems and autonomous irrigation equipment enhance precision while lowering labour and operating costs. AI helps water resource management by enhancing drought prediction, leak detection, and fair water distribution.
- Infrastructure, data accessibility, technical know-how, and fair access continue to be issues, particularly for smallholder farmers.
- Edge AI, robotics integration, climate-adaptive models, and the democratization of AI tools are future trends that will increase the effectiveness and accessibility of intelligent water management on a worldwide scale.

Observing the Future:

In light of water shortage and climate change, AI-driven agricultural water management will be essential to supplying the world's expanding food needs. To fully realize AI's promise and ensure sustainable farming methods that preserve water supplies and promote global food security, more innovation, funding, and inclusive regulations are needed.

Chapter 6: Using AI to Manage Diseases and Detect Pests

Overview: The Unseen Threats to Agriculture

The Food and Agriculture Organization (FAO) estimates that *up to 40% of the world's food production is destroyed annually by pests and crop diseases*. Fall Armyworm, Desert Locusts, and Maize Lethal Necrosis have severely reduced the yields of staple crops in Africa alone, endangering the food security of millions of people.

Historically, visual scouting, blanket pesticide applications, and manual record-keeping have been the mainstays of pest and disease control. Intervention in the late stages

Because of labour shortages, pesticide resistance, and climate change, these approaches are reactive, inefficient, and becoming less and less successful. AI now provides a more intelligent, quick, and accurate solution.

6.1. How AI Combats Pests and Plant Disease

Crop protection benefits from AI's automation, intelligence, and predictive capabilities. Here's how:

1. **Using Computer Vision to Identify Diseases**

   AI systems can examine images of leaves, stems, or fruits using deep learning-powered image recognition to diagnose:

   - Mosaic virus,
   - rust,
   - bacterial spots,
   - blight,
   - Powdery mildew, and more.

To identify diseases based on changes in colour, texture, and pattern, these models are trained on hundreds of annotated photos.

1. **Using Computer Vision to Identify Diseases**

   AI systems can examine images of leaves, stems, or fruits using deep learning.

1. **Identification and Counting of Pests**

   Drones and field cameras with AI capabilities can:

   - Identify different pest species (such as beetles, aphids, and caterpillars);
   - Monitor their movements and population dynamics; and

- Notify farmers before infestations reach financial thresholds.

1. **Systems of Early Warning**

Artificial intelligence (AI) models use satellite data, weather forecasts, and insect migration patterns to anticipate outbreaks days or even weeks before they happen.

1. **Treatment Predictive Analytics**

Based on past effectiveness, machine learning algorithms advocate biological control techniques and only recommend targeted pesticide administration where necessary.

1. **Apps for Scouting Driven by AI**

Farmers can enter observations or upload photos using mobile apps. AI provides the following responses:

- Diagnosis, severity degree, and suggested courses of action.
- Alerts on nearby outbreaks from linked farms

6.1.2. Study Case No. 1: PlantVillage Africa's Nuru

Nuru, an AI helper created by Penn State University and FAO, uses computer vision to identify:

- Cassava mosaic
- Fall armyworm;
- Lethal necrosis of maize

Even offline, Nuru provides an immediate diagnostic when farmers merely aim their smartphone at a plant. With 90% diagnosis accuracy, more than 60,000 farmers in ten African nations have utilized it.

6.1.3. Case Study 2: Taranis (Ukraine, Brazil, and the United States)

Taranis monitors thousands of acres using high-resolution photography and drones powered by AI. Its algorithms identify:

- Hotspots for pests; stress on nutrients; and outbreaks of weeds and fungi

Results:

- Significant decrease in pesticide use;
- Up to 20% increase in yield;
- Real-time alerts enable prompt, localized intervention

6.1.4. Case Study 3: The Plantix App by PEAT (India/Germany)

More than 10 million farmers use Plantix, which uses CNNs to:

- Identify more than 500 crop diseases;
- Provide location-based treatment recommendations; and
- Create heat maps of outbreaks throughout the community.

In Southeast Asia, Brazil, and India, smallholder farmers now carry around a digital agronomist in their pockets.

6.1.5. Drones with AI and Robotic Scouting

When equipped with multispectral cameras and edge AI chips, autonomous drones and rovers can:

- Map infection zones at the plant level;
- Monitor fields every day;
- Identify minute indications of illness (such as colour shift or leaf curling);

Early detection—before symptoms are apparent to humans—is made possible by these robotic scouts.

6.2. The Weather and Environment's Role

AI combines climate data with models of pests and diseases:

- In pathogen/pest lifecycle modelling, temperature, humidity, and wind patterns are important factors.
- Using patterns in humidity and rainfall frequency, AI may forecast fungal epidemics.
- AI-enhanced satellite imagery is being used to follow locust swarms, directing international cooperation and ground spraying operations.

6.2.1. Diagram: AI's Advantages for Managing Diseases and Pests

Impact	**Benefits**
Early Detection	Finds problems before they cause financial harm.
Precision Treatment	Lessens the environmental impact and use of pesticides.
Yield Protection	Reduces losses and increases crop yield while saving labour.
Labour Savings	Takes the place of laborious manual scouting.
Data-Driven Decisions	Permits traceability and evidence-based responses.
Cost Reduction	Reduces needless effort, crop losses, and spraying.

Figure 9: AI's Advantages for Managing Diseases and Pests

6.3. Obstacles and Deficits

Adoption has challenges despite its advantages:

- Rare or developing disease datasets are limited;
- local image training is required (regional diseases frequently lack picture libraries);
- Connectivity problems prevent real-time drone or app use; and high-resolution cameras and sensors are expensive.

There are initiatives to:

- Create publicly available image databases for worldwide pest identification;
- Include offline AI inference in rural applications; and
- Use national agricultural extension organizations as distribution channels.

6.4. Future Directions: Biosecurity Driven by AI

1. **Monitoring of Pathogens in Real Time**

Soon, genomic AI will use biosensors to identify pathogens in the field, identifying illnesses before symptoms show up.

1. **Heatmaps of Disease Worldwide**

Live disease maps will be made available by integrated AI platforms, which will direct cross-border crop protection, food policy, and international trade.

1. **Self-governing Drones for Pesticides**

AI-guided drones will precisely spray biopesticide microdoses, reducing expenses and residue.

1. **Contracts for Disease Forecasting**

Using AI-driven triggers, smart contracts will tie insurance pay-outs to anticipated pest or disease outbreaks.

1. **Models of Integrated Pests and Diseases**

In order to suggest comprehensive solutions, unified models will replicate ecosystem-level interactions between crops, pests, predators, and climate.

In conclusion, Crop protection used to require observation, anticipation, and response. AI now gives farmers the ability to anticipate, stop, and safeguard. Crops, expenses, and ecosystems are all being saved by this change from reactive to proactive pest and disease management.

A future of agriculture where insect outbreaks are uncommon and swiftly eliminated with little collateral harm is promised by the convergence of artificial intelligence, robotics, imaging, and biological research.

We'll examine how satellite integration and big data are offering farmers a bird's-eye perspective and enabling them to see, plan, and act at scale in the upcoming chapter.

Chapter 7: Integration of Big Data and Satellites in Farm Management

Overview: A New Age of Understanding

Digital agriculture has advanced significantly with the combination of satellite technology and Big Data analytics. Farmers no longer rely only on seasonal intuition or physical field inspections.

With the advent of the digital age, traditional agriculture has changed into a precision-focused, data-driven sector. The key to this change is the effective fusion of satellite technology and big data analytics, which are transforming farm management. This chapter examines how farmers may now obtain previously unheard-of insights regarding their land, crops, and environmental conditions thanks to these cutting-edge equipment, bringing about a new era of knowledge.

Big data, which includes vast amounts of information from many sources like satellite imaging, weather stations, machinery, and soil sensors, is being used to make prompt, well-informed judgments. Continuous, extensive, and real-time observations of agricultural landscapes are made possible by satellites in high orbit. Together, these technologies give farmers access to accurate, useful information that maximizes agricultural productivity, resource efficiency, and sustainability.

The foundation of contemporary smart farming is the combination of big data and satellites, which can be used for everything from tracking soil moisture and nutrient levels to forecasting pest outbreaks and weather patterns. By lowering waste and the ecological impact of agriculture, this synergy promotes environmental stewardship in addition to increasing productivity and profitability.

These days, they may use massive data streams—gathered from IoT sensors, weather stations, and market reports—and real-time, high-resolution satellite imagery to make data-driven decisions that improve profitability, sustainability, and productivity.

This chapter will examine the technologies that make this integration possible, its main advantages, implementation difficulties, and emerging trends influencing the field of farm management. Greetings from the new era of agricultural knowledge, where satellites and data collaborate to create farms that are more intelligent and resilient.

7.1. Big Data's Function in Agriculture

Large, varied collections of data, both organized and unstructured, that are too complicated for conventional data processing software are referred to as "*big data.*" Big Data in agriculture comes from a variety of sources, including: IoT-enabled machinery (such as tractors and irrigation systems); soil and moisture sensors; historical and current weather patterns; crop health indicators; market trends, and logistics.

Big data has become a key component of contemporary agriculture, revolutionizing the way farmers gather, examine, and use enormous volumes of data to improve sustainability and productivity. Big data basically refers to very huge datasets that, with the right processing and analysis, provide insightful patterns, trends, and information that are not visible through small-scale data collection or traditional observation.

7.1.1. Sources of Big Data in Agriculture

Big data about agriculture is collected from many different sources, such as:

- Soil sensors that measure temperature, pH, moisture content, and nutrient content.
- Local and regional weather forecasts are provided by weather stations and climate models; farm machinery telemetry records equipment performance and usage trends.
- High-resolution images of crop health and growth stages are provided via satellite and drone imaging.
- Supply chain and market data that aids in demand forecasting and sales optimization

7.1.2. The Applications of Big Data in Agriculture

Analysing large data using complex algorithms and machine learning models is where its real strength lies. Using historical and real-time data, these technologies allow farmers and agribusinesses to:

- Predict crop yields;
- Optimize irrigation and fertilization schedules to maximize growth while conserving resources;
- Monitor soil health and modify crop rotations accordingly;
- Improve risk management by foreseeing unfavourable weather events and market fluctuations;
- Improve decision-making with data-driven insights rather than depending solely on experience or intuition.

7.1.3. Big Data's Advantages for Agriculture

There are numerous important advantages of using big data in farming.

- **Enhanced Productivity**: Accurate resource allocation made possible by data-driven farming techniques increases crop yield per hectare.
- **Cost Effectiveness**: Waste is decreased and operating expenses are decreased through optimal use of inputs (water, fertilizer, and insecticides).
- **Sustainability:** Ecologically friendly farming methods are supported by a deeper comprehension of ecosystem dynamics.
- **Resilience:** Farmers may better plan for and reduce the risks associated with pests and climate change by using predictive analytics.

7.1.4. Obstacles and Things to Think About

Despite its potential, there are obstacles to big data integration in agriculture, including issues with data accessibility and quality, the digital gap among farmers, privacy concerns, and the requirement for user-friendly platforms that convert complex data into insights that can be put to use.

7.2. Satellite Technology

With satellite technology, farmers can now see their fields from above and conduct previously unfeasible large-scale surveillance, making it an essential tool in modern agriculture. Satellites provide vital information that enables precision farming and more intelligent decision-making by gathering high-resolution photos and data over large geographic areas.

7.2.1. Satellite Data Types for Agriculture

Agricultural satellites gather a variety of information that is essential to farm management, such as:

- **Multispectral And Hyper-spectral Imagery**: By capturing light that is not visible to the human eye, these pictures provide information about soil conditions, water stress, and plant health that is not visible to the human eye.
- **Synthetic Aperture Radar (SAR):** This day-and-night tool, which can penetrate clouds, is helpful for tracking crop structure, surface roughness, and soil moisture.
- **Thermal Imaging:** Detects temperature fluctuations that can signal irrigation demands, pest infestations, or disease outbreaks.
- **Geolocation and Mapping Data**: Aids in logistics and planning by providing precise field boundaries.

7.2.2. **Satellite Technology Applications in Agriculture**

Many agricultural applications are made possible by satellites:

- **Crop Monitoring**: Frequent imaging aids in estimating biomass and production, identifying stressed areas, and evaluating crop health.

- **Analysis of Soil and Moisture**: Satellite data monitors irrigation efficiency and soil moisture content, facilitating improved water management.
- **Detection of Pests and Diseases**: Variations in plant reflectance patterns can be used to identify early indicators of infestations or diseases.
- **Disaster Management**: By monitoring floods, droughts, and other environmental stressors, satellites facilitate prompt reaction and recovery.
- **Land Use Planning:** Decisions about crop rotation, land distribution, and sustainable farming methods are aided by mapping and classification.

7.2.3. Satellite Technology Benefits

- **Broad Coverage:** Satellites are perfect for monitoring farms of all sizes because they can reach far-flung locations.
- **Regular Revisits:** Timely interventions are made possible by the daily or nearly daily information that many satellites offer.
- **Non-Invasive**: No crops or soil are disturbed during data collecting.
- **Integration:** For all-encompassing farm management, satellite data can be integrated with information from sensors, drones, and weather stations.

7.2.4. Obstacles And Restrictions

- **Limits of Resolution**: Even though satellite imaging is getting better, it occasionally lacks the fine detail that drones or ground sensors can provide.
- **Weather and Cloud Cover**: Although radar systems help

to alleviate this problem, clouds can impede optical satellite data.

- **Data Processing**: To convert raw satellite data into useful insights, a great deal of processing and experience are needed.
- **Cost and Accessibility**: Smallholder farmers may not be able to obtain certain high-resolution data sets due to their high cost or restrictions.

7.3. Integration Model: How Satellite Data Feeds Big Data Systems

When big data systems and satellite data come together to produce a smooth integration model that turns unprocessed observations into useful intelligence, the full potential of contemporary farm management becomes apparent. Through this integration, satellite-derived insights are fed into extensive big data platforms, empowering farmers to make accurate, data-driven decisions.

7.3.1. **Data Collection and Flow**

A vast range of data is continuously captured by satellite systems, ranging from temperature fluctuations and soil moisture levels to multispectral images showing crop health. This information is sent to cloud-based platforms and ground sensors, where it joins the larger agricultural big data ecosystem.

At this point, other data streams are integrated with satellite data, such as:

- Historical crop yield and planting data;
- Weather forecasts and real-time climate data;
- Machinery and equipment telemetry;
- Soil sensor readings (pH, moisture, and nutrients); and
- Market and supply chain data.

These inputs work together to create a complete data repository that is necessary for thorough farm analysis.

7.3.2. **Analytics and Data Processing**

After being included into big data platforms, satellite data is processed through several layers:

- **Pre-processing** is the process of removing atmospheric distortion, sensor noise, and misalignment with geographic coordinates from satellite images.

- **Feature extraction:** Finding important variables like thermal hotspots, soil moisture anomalies, or vegetation indices (such as the Normalized Difference Vegetation Index, or NDVI).
- **Integration:** Contextual accuracy is achieved by combining ground-based data with satellite features.
- **Modelling and Prediction:** Using AI and machine learning algorithms to estimate yields, crop stress, disease outbreaks, and the best times to harvest.
- **Visualization:** Displaying results in a way that farmers and agronomists can understand, such as dashboards, maps, and alarms.

7.3.3. Farm Management Feedback Loop

The integration model has ongoing feedback loops and is not a one-way data pipeline:

- **Data Validation**: By confirming and offering ground truth input on insights obtained from satellites, farmers can increase the accuracy of models.
- **Adaptive Management**: Certain actions, such targeted fertilization, irrigation, or pest control, are prompted by insights.
- **Constant Observation**: Satellites frequently deliver updated data, enabling modifications in response to changing field circumstances.

7.3.4. The Integration Model's Advantages

- **Precision:** Enables precise decision-making by fusing micro-level ground data with the macro-level viewpoint of satellites.

- **Scalability:** Fits farms of all sizes, from small-scale farms to massive commercial enterprises.
- **Timeliness:** Quick data updates allow for timely reactions to new opportunities or dangers.
- **Resource Optimization**: By only applying treatments where and when necessary, input waste is reduced.

7.3.5. Obstacles and Things to Think About

- **Data Interoperability:** It's critical to guarantee compatibility across various data types and systems.
- **Infrastructure:** In remote places, access to dependable internet and cloud computing resources may be a challenge.
- **Expertise:** To understand and act upon insights from integrated data, farmers and agronomists need to be trained.
- **Security and Privacy**: Preserving trust requires safeguarding private agricultural data from abuse.

7.4. Case Study 1: Ukrainian Agriculture and SpaceKnow

SpaceKnow monitored agricultural activity in Ukraine during wartime disturbances using AI and satellite photos. Their technology helped the government and non-governmental organizations plan food security measures by tracking planted areas, estimating yields, and flagging inactive zones.

Key Takeaway: National and international food policy are influenced by satellite big data analytics, which is not just for farmers.

7.5. Case Study 2: Climate Corporation (US)

Climate Corp, which is owned by Bayer, generates field health maps and yield estimates for farmers in the US Midwest by integrating meteorological forecasts, satellite imagery, and field-level data.

Impacts Include:

- A 15% increase in maize output in pilot regions;
- A 25% decrease in fertilizer waste; and
- Farmers receiving notifications about certain field zones that require attention.

7.6. African Use Case: Zambia and India Using Digital Green + SatSure

SatSure, a satellite data analytics company, and Digital Green, a non-profit agri-tech organization, work together to provide smallholder farmers with useful insights via cellphones. In Zambia, food security and resilience are increased by using satellite data to determine when to sow maize based on patterns in soil moisture and rainfall.

7.6.1. Diagram: Big Data and Satellite Integration in Farm Management

Figure 10: Big Data and Satellite Integration in Farm Management

7.6.1. Diagram: Advantages of Satellite Integration and Big Data

Benefit	Description
Improved Yield Forecasting	Planning for storage, insurance, and logistics is guided by precise seasonal output estimates.
Efficiency Resource Allocation	Determine the water and nutrient requirements for each zone in real time.
Risk Management	Losses are decreased by early warning systems for illnesses, pests, and droughts.
Sustainability	Allows for less chemical runoff, precision irrigation, and conservation tillage.
Market Intelligence	Adapt production to changes in pricing and demand.

Figure 11: Advantages of Satellite Integration and Big Data

7.6.2. Diagram: Difficulties and Restrictions

Challenge	Implication
Data Overload	Without the right training, farmers could find it difficult to understand complex datasets.
Cost and Accessibility	Smallholder farmers might not have access to data platforms and satellites.
Internet & Power Dependency	Reliable digital infrastructure is frequently lacking in rural areas.
Data Privacy Concerns	There are still problems with farm-level data ownership and usage.

Figure 12: Difficulties and Restrictions

7.9. Future Directions: Where Are We Going?

Big data and satellite technology integration in farm management is set to develop into increasingly more complex and significant systems as technology continues to progress at a breakneck rate. The future is full of exciting opportunities that could improve sustainability, expand our knowledge of agricultural ecosystems, and give farmers all across the world more power.

7.9.1. Improved Satellite Capabilities

Better geographical, spectral, and temporal resolution will be available on upcoming satellite missions, allowing for even more frequent and in-depth crop and soil condition monitoring. In order to respond quickly to crop stress and climatic changes, smaller satellites and satellite constellations will boost revisit rates to near real-time observations.

7.9.2. Developments in AI and Machine Learning

7.9.3. In the analysis of intricate agricultural datasets, artificial intelligence will become more and more important. *In order to provide incredibly precise forecasts and customized suggestions, more sophisticated models will use data from multiple sources, including satellite imagery, drone footage, IoT sensor outputs, and market trends.* Farmers with different degrees of technical expertise will be able to benefit from these AI systems as they become easier to operate.

7.9.4. Connectivity with Additional Emerging Technologies

- **Internet of Things (IoT):** By combining satellite data with extensive on-field sensor networks, hyper-localized insights for targeted actions will be produced.
- **Blockchain:** Improving agricultural supply chains' traceability, transparency, and data security.
- **Edge Computing**: lowering latency and facilitating real-

time decision-making, even in faraway locations, by processing data closer to the source.

7.9.5. Sustainable and Climate-Resilient Agriculture

The development of climate change-adaptive farming methods will heavily rely on big data and satellite technologies. Farmers will be able to plan for extreme weather events, maximize resource utilization, and apply regenerative agriculture practices that improve biodiversity and soil health with the aid of predictive analytics.

7.9.6. Democratization of Data Access

Smallholder and resource-constrained farmers will be able to take advantage of these technologies thanks to initiatives to reduce costs and increase accessibility. Mobile apps, open data projects, and cloud platforms will close digital gaps and promote equitable growth and food security.

7.9.7. Considerations of Ethics and Policy

Policies pertaining to data ownership, privacy, and ethical use will become more crucial as data-driven agriculture grows. The proper development of farm management technologies will be shaped by frameworks that uphold farmers' rights and promote innovation.

The path to a more intelligent and sustainable agricultural future has begun. *Farmers and other stakeholders may foster production, efficiency, and resilience by embracing the integration of big data and satellite technologies, guaranteeing food security for future generations.*

In conclusion, there is no longer any limit to the sky. Farming is now a predictive science rather than a reactive activity because to the combination of Big Data and satellite integration. The smallest farms in the most isolated villages will soon be able to use data and space to grow more with less thanks to the ongoing democratization of these technologies through legislation, education, and mobile access.

Chapter 8: AI-Powered Livestock Feeding and Monitoring Systems

Overview: Ingenious Farming Outside of the Fields

Although *Crop Production* is the primary focus of agricultural innovation, AI-powered tools are making livestock management a lot more accurate and effective activity. *The way farmers care for their animals is being revolutionized by intelligent feeding systems, health monitoring, and behavioural analysis, which ensures increased sustainability, welfare, and productivity.* Livestock farming is evolving beyond conventional techniques by utilizing sensors, IoT devices, and AI algorithms to provide automated care and real-time insights that maximize resource utilization and minimize losses.

Fixed feeding schedules, manual observation, and human intuition are no longer the only aspects of livestock farming. *AI-enabled livestock monitoring and intelligent feeding systems are transforming animal husbandry in the Age of Agriculture 4.0 by boosting productivity, ensuring sustainable practices, optimizing feed utilization, and increasing animal health.*

Artificial Intelligence (AI) analyses cattle behaviour, health, nutrition, and environmental factors using real-time data from wearable sensors, cameras, and connected devices. AI provides insightful information that helps make decisions automatically or with little help from humans.

8.1. Important Elements of AI-Powered Livestock Systems

8.1.1. Diagram: Important Elements of AI-Powered Livestock Systems

Component	Function
Wearable IoT Sensors	Monitor the location, activity, temperature, heart rate, and rumination of the animal.
Computer Vision Systems	Recognize social contact, feeding habits, lameness, and posture.
Automated Feeders	Use AI-generated recommendations to dispense the appropriate amount of feed.
Cloud-Based AI Platforms	Examine data trends and send out notifications in real time.
Drones & Robots	Utilized for feeding or supplement delivery, herd monitoring, and counting.

Figure 13: Important Elements of AI-Powered Livestock Systems

8.2. AI Applications in Livestock Farming

8.2.1. Early Disease Detection and Health Monitoring

Artificial intelligence (AI) models examine sensor and behavioural data to detect:

- Abnormal movements (cattle lameness, for example)
- Sudden temperature decreases (potential disease)
- Modifications to water or feed input

For instance, an AI system can identify a possible case of mastitis before physical signs show up by identifying a cow that is less mobile and has a higher body temperature. This allows for early treatment and stops the disease from spreading.

8.2.2. Systems for Intelligent Feeding

AI-powered feeding programs assess each animal's requirements according to its species, age, weight, and overall health. By precisely dispensing feed, automated feeders increase nutrition efficiency and reduce waste. In order to support growth, reproduction, and the production of milk or meat, machine learning algorithms forecast feeding behaviour and dynamically modify feeds.

8.2.3. Disease Detection and Health Monitoring

Vital indications including temperature, heart rate, and activity level are monitored by wearable sensors and smart cameras. AI systems examine departures from typical patterns to identify early indicators of disease or stress. Timely measures resulting from early disease diagnosis lower veterinarian expenses and stop epidemics.

8.2.4. Welfare-Based Behavioural Analysis

To evaluate an animal's well-being, artificial intelligence (AI) systems track its movements, social connections, and eating habits. By identifying abnormalities, farmers can improve animal wellbeing by addressing issues like pain, discomfort, or unfavourable environmental conditions.

8.2.5. Automated Data Integration and Record-Keeping

Farmers are given a thorough picture of their herds thanks to the integration of data from multiple sensors into centralized platforms. Dashboards driven by AI offer predictive analytics and actionable information for productivity optimization, breeding choices, and herd management.

8.2.6. Prospects for the Future: Toward Completely Self-Sufficiency Livestock Farms

Fully autonomous systems that integrate robotics, drones, and AI to control feeding, security, cleaning, and health monitoring are part of the future of AI in livestock farming. These developments hold promise for lowering labour intensity while significantly enhancing sustainability and animal welfare.

8.3. Key Components of Livestock Systems Driven by AI

For AI-powered livestock feeding and monitoring systems to provide precise, real-time data and automatic responses, a number of essential parts must function flawlessly together. To fully appreciate how AI turns conventional livestock farming into a precision-driven, effective enterprise, it is imperative to comprehend these components.

8.3.1. IoT Devices And Sensors

A network of sensors and Internet of Things (IoT) devices forms the foundation of any AI livestock system. These include motion detectors, rumen boluses, wearable collars, ear tags, and environmental sensors that continuously gather information on the health of the animals (heart rate, temperature), their behaviour (movement, grazing habits), and their environment (humidity, temperature, air quality).

8.3.2. Data Collection and Transmission

These devices send data wirelessly to cloud computing platforms or central processing units. For real-time monitoring and decision-making, dependable connectivity—whether over Wi-Fi, Bluetooth, LoRaWAN, or cellular networks—is essential, particularly in distant agricultural areas.

8.3.3. Management and Storage of Data

Large data sets necessitate reliable storage options, frequently cloud-based, that guarantee data security, scalability, and accessibility. To preserve accuracy and privacy, proper data management involves organizing, cleansing, and anonymizing data.

8.3.4. Algorithms for AI and Machine Learning

Incoming data is analysed by sophisticated algorithms to find trends, forecast health problems, and improve feeding schedules. Adaptive and customized livestock management is made possible by machine learning models that are trained on both historical and current data to increase accuracy over time.

8.3.5. Mechanized Feeding Systems

Actuators in intelligent feeders dispense precisely the right amount of feed based on each animal's nutritional requirements in response to AI-generated commands. By doing this, waste is decreased and ideal growth and production are guaranteed.

8.3.6. Tools for Decision Support and User Interface

Dashboards and smartphone apps that provide insights, warnings, and suggestions in an easy-to-understand manner are how farmers communicate with AI systems. These interfaces facilitate resource allocation, strategic planning, and prompt interventions.

8.3.7. Farm Management System Integration

In order to provide comprehensive farm optimization, AI livestock systems frequently interface with larger farm management platforms, integrating information from crops, weather forecasts, and market trends.

8.3.8. Measures for Security and Privacy

It's critical to defend private farm data against online attacks. To protect data, systems use secure data transfer protocols, user authentication, and encryption.

8.4. Using AI in Livestock Production

Through the introduction of clever solutions that enhance animal health, production, and farm sustainability, artificial intelligence is quickly changing the livestock farming industry. The following are some important areas where AI is having a big influence.

8.4.1. Accurate Nutrition Management and Feeding

AI systems customize feeding schedules and rations by analysing data on each animal's weight, growth rate, and nutritional needs. By guaranteeing ideal nutrient intake, this accuracy decreases expenses, minimizes feed waste, and enhances overall animal performance.

8.4.2. Early Disease Detection and Health Monitoring

Wearable technology and cameras driven by AI continuously track behaviour and vital signs to identify indicators of illness or distress early. By detecting minor changes, machine learning models allow for timely treatment that lowers mortality rates and stops the spread of disease.

8.4.3. Breeding Optimization And Reproductive Management

In order to suggest the ideal time for breeding and choosing high-performing cattle, AI systems monitor oestrous cycles, reproductive markers, and genetic characteristics. Over time, this improves herd quality and maximizes reproduction rates.

8.4.4. Using Behaviour Analysis to Evaluate Welfare

AI uses sensor data and video analytics to identify shifts in social contact, feeding, and activity patterns. Early detection of stress or pain enables farmers to enhance environmental, handling, or housing circumstances, so improving animal welfare.

8.4.5. Security and Surveillance Automation

Drones and smart cameras driven by AI keep an eye on cattle enclosures, looking for predators, unauthorized entry, or attempts at escape. In large-scale operations, this lowers manpower requirements while improving security.

8.4.6. Reduction of Environmental Impact

AI systems minimize greenhouse gas emissions and nutrient runoff by optimizing feed efficiency and manure management. Eco-friendly farming is facilitated by AI-supported sustainable methods.

8.4.7. Farm Management Predictive Analytics

AI helps farmers plan feeding, sales, and resource allocation for maximum profitability by combining weather, feed availability, and market price data to generate forecasts and suggestions.

8.5. Precision Feeding Systems

AI and cutting-edge technology are used by precision feeding systems to provide each animal with the proper amount and kind of feed according to its particular requirements. In livestock production, these approaches maximize nutrition, reduce waste, and raise total productivity.

8.5.1. Important Elements of Accurate Feeding Systems:

- **Individual Animal Monitoring**: The system continuously monitors each animal's weight, growth rate, health, and feeding habits using sensors and RFID tags. Customized feeding plans are based on this data.
- **Automated Feed Dispensers**: The AI system is linked to intelligent feeders that precisely dispense feed amounts for each animal. AI-driven analysis enables these dispensers to dynamically modify meals.
- **Nutritional Optimization**: AI algorithms examine gathered data to create feed mixtures that are ideal for the animals' nutritional needs while taking age, reproductive state, and production objectives (e.g., weight gain, milk yield) into consideration.
- **Waste Reduction:** Precision feeding systems drastically cut feed waste by just providing what each animal need, which lowers expenses and has a positive environmental impact.
- **Integration with Farm Management Platforms:** Farmers may track feed consumption trends, modify their approaches, and enhance herd performance by integrating precision feeding data with more comprehensive farm management platforms.

8.5.2. Benefits

- Reduced environmental impact due to less waste and overfeeding;
- Increased animal health and production;
- Increased feed efficiency and cost savings; and
- Real-time adaptation to shifting environmental circumstances or animal needs.

8.5.3. Breeding Optimization

By facilitating data-driven decisions that improve genetic quality, reproductive efficiency, and overall herd productivity, artificial intelligence (AI) technologies are transforming livestock breeding. Breeding optimization tools let farmers choose the best animals for reproduction and precisely manage breeding cycles by using machine learning and advanced analytics.

8.5.3.1. Important Elements of AI-Powered Breeding Optimization:

- **Genetic Analysis and Selection**: AI systems examine phenotypic characteristics including growth rates, milk output, and illness resistance in addition to genomic data. This all-encompassing method speeds up genetic improvement within herds by assisting in the identification of animals with the most desired genetic profiles.
- **Oestrus Detection and Fertility Monitoring**: In real time, behavioural monitoring systems and wearable sensors track fertility indicators and oestrus (heat) indicators. These data points are processed by AI models to forecast the best times for breeding, which raises conception rates and decreases lost opportunities.
- **Breeding Decision Support:** AI uses environmental, genetic, and health data to suggest mating couples that minimize the danger of inbreeding while maximizing desired features. This guarantees more resilient and productive herds with sustainable growth.
- **Predictive Reproductive Management**: Proactive measures that improve pregnancy success and animal comfort are made possible by machine learning models that

predict reproductive outcomes and possible difficulties.

- **Benefits include:**
    - Enhanced animal health and longevity through wise breeding decisions;
    - Accelerated genetic improvement and higher-quality progeny;
    - Decreased breeding costs and labour through automation; and
    - Increased reproductive efficiency and herd production.

8.5.3.2. Comprehending Behaviour

AI-powered livestock management relies heavily on behavioural analysis, which provides deep insights into animal welfare, health, and productivity. By continuously tracking and analysing the movements, social interactions, and activity patterns of animals, AI systems assist farmers in identifying problems early and optimizing living conditions.

Key Features of AI-Driven Behavioural Understanding:

- **Movement and Activity Monitoring:** Cameras and sensors record daily movement patterns, grazing habits, and rest periods; deviations from normal activity can indicate pain, illness, or environmental stress;
- **Social Interaction Analysis:** AI assesses how animals interact within the herd, identifying aggression, isolation, or changes in social hierarchy; these insights guide management decisions that enhance animal welfare and minimize injuries.

- **Feeding Behaviour Tracking:** By keeping an eye on feeding schedules and consumption trends, one might identify problems with digestion, discomfort, or resource competition.
- **Early Stress and Discomfort Detection**: AI may notify farmers of early indicators of stress brought on by handling, disease, or environmental variables by examining tiny behavioural clues. This allows for prompt intervention.
- **Benefits** include:
    - Increased output by keeping healthy, stress-free animals;
    - Decreased disease outbreaks by identifying early symptoms; and
    - Improved animal welfare through proactive care.

Data-driven environmental modifications to maximize performance and comfort.

8.6. Case Study 1: The IDA System from Connecterra (Netherlands)

Connecterra created the AI platform IDA (Intelligent Dairy Assistant), which combines wearable sensors on dairy cows with machine learning:

- Provides actionable advise (e.g., vet call, insemination time);
- Sends alerts via mobile app;
- Detects lameness, oestrus, calving, and feeding behaviour.

Impacts include

- a 50% decrease in the use of antibiotics and
- A 33% increase in reproductive cycle detection.
- Increased profitability and welfare of the herd.

8.7. Case Study 2: Cainthus Computer Vision (USA)

Cainthus monitors feed bunk occupancy, drinking habits, and cow lying/resting hours in barns using AI-powered cameras. AI identifies anomalies by comparing observed actions to ideal norms.

Result: In order to facilitate quicker interventions, farmers receive a dashboard report that identifies animals that are underfed or stressed.

8.8. African Setting: AI-Driven Livestock Health in Kenyan

The "Smart Brooder," created by start-ups like Arinifu, employs sensors and artificial intelligence to control lighting, humidity, and temperature in chicken habitats.

Additionally, Zenvus Livestock is developing a wearable AI system that uses smartphone apps and solar-powered sensors to detect movement, grazing patterns, and animal health for pastoralists in Africa.

Benefit: Lowers losses from disease, theft, and inadequate nutrition in isolated locations with little access to veterinarians.

8.8.1. Diagram: Advantages of AI for Livestock Systems

Benefit	Description
Healthier Animals	Targeted care, less stress, and early disease detect
Improved Productivity	Increased success in reproduction, quicker growth rates, and improved feed efficiency.
Labour Efficiency	Human mistake and manual work are decreased by automated monitoring.
Sustainability	Minimized environmental impact and optimal use of resources (feed, water, and energy)
Animal Welfare	Better living conditions as a result of data-driven administration

Figure 14: Advantages of AI for Livestock Systems

8.8.2. Diagram: Implementation Challenges

Challenge	**Explanation**
Cost of Technology	For small-scale farmers, wearable technology and AI platforms can be costly.
Internet and Power Dependence	The infrastructure needed for real-time data processing may be lacking in rural locations.
Data Overload	To understand and act upon AI-generated insights, farmers could require training.
Cultural Adoption	High-tech interventions may be resisted by traditional cattle methods.

Figure 15: Implementation Challenges

8.9. Prospects for AI-Livestock Integration in the Future

AI has the potential to revolutionize livestock farming in the future by converting conventional methods into extremely effective, sustainable, and animal-friendly systems. In order to create smart farms that function with the least amount of human interaction and the highest productivity, emerging technologies and continuing breakthroughs promise to further integrate AI, robotics, and data analytics.

Among the main prospects are:

- **Fully Autonomous Livestock Farms:** Thanks to developments in robotics and artificial intelligence, farms will be able to manage security, cleaning, feeding, and health monitoring on their own. Precision handling of everyday tasks by robots could lower labour needs and increase consistency.
- **Livestock Digital Twins:** Construct a "digital twin" or real-time virtual model of every animal that replicates its behaviour, metabolism, and overall health to enable virtual testing of feeding or treatment plans.
- **Real-Time Health and Genetic Management:** By combining AI with genetic sequencing and ongoing health monitoring, breeding, feeding, and care can be adjusted in real-time, improving the resilience and productivity of herds.
- **Improved Environmental Sustainability:** By maximizing feed efficiency, waste management, and resource consumption, artificial intelligence (AI) will be important in reducing the environmental impact of cattle farming and advancing climate-smart agriculture.

- **AI-Driven Decision Ecosystems:** These systems will combine supply chain logistics, market trends, weather forecasts, and animal data to give farmers all the information they need to make informed decisions that will optimize sustainability and profitability.
- **Robotic Herding and Monitoring Driven by AI**: Fully autonomous drones and ground robots will guide animals to feeding or milking stations, monitor and herd cattle over vast fields, and identify sickness.
- **Personalized Animal Care:** Farms will create care plans specifically for each animal based on behavioural and physiological data powered by AI, enhancing welfare and lowering productivity losses brought on by stress. AI will combine health history and genomes to create customized feeding schedules for valuable cattle, such dairy champions or breeding bulls.
- **Blockchain and Data Transparency**: By combining AI and blockchain technology, the livestock supply chain may become more transparent and traceable, ensuring that consumers are assured of high-quality products and moral agricultural methods. In order to ensure food safety and compliance in the global meat and dairy markets, AI systems will connect with blockchain to track each animal's health, diet, medicine, and movement history.
- **Sound Diagnostics and Voice Recognition**: Soon, artificial intelligence (AI) algorithms will analyse animal speech patterns—particularly in pigs and poultry—to detect stress, illness, or pain.

Challenges and Considerations: Although encouraging, issues like high upfront investment costs, data privacy concerns, farmer training, and infrastructure development—particularly in poor nations—will need to be addressed before widespread adoption can occur.

8.9.1. Diagram: AI-Enabled Livestock Monitoring and Feeding Systems

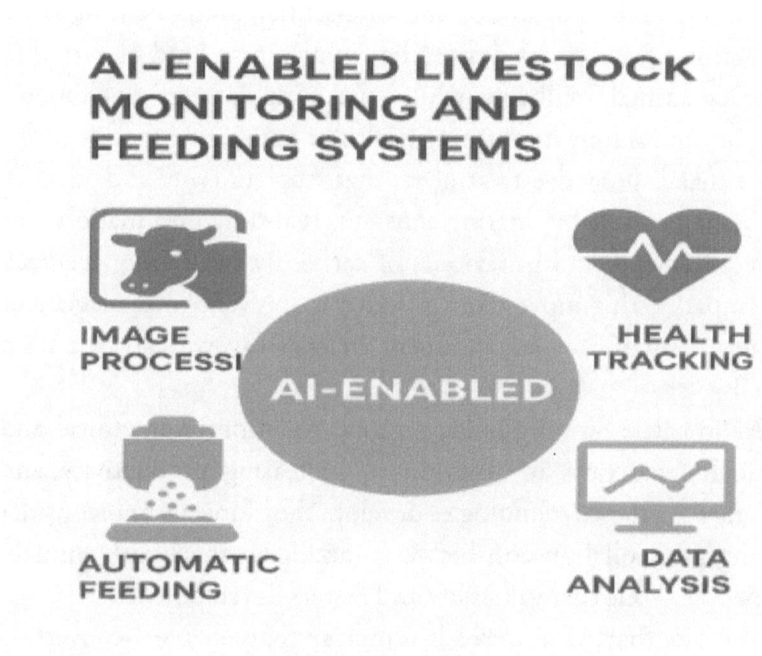

Figure 16: AI-Enabled Livestock Monitoring and Feeding Systems

8.10. Final Thoughts: Intelligence That Cares

The combination of technology and empathy becomes a distinguishing characteristic of contemporary agriculture as AI-powered technologies become an essential component of cattle production. These smart devices represent a new kind of care that improves animal wellbeing while sustaining farmers' livelihoods, going beyond simply monitoring health or optimizing food.

AI makes proactive treatments that stop suffering and advance well-being possible by offering constant, real-time information into the requirements and behaviours of cattle. By combining accuracy and empathy, this move from reactive to preventive management signifies a significant advancement in the way we care for farm animals.

AI in cattle farming holds promise for promoting ethical and sustainable practices in addition to increasing productivity and efficiency. As these technologies develop, they force us to reconsider farming as a collaboration between intelligent machines, animals, and people—one that values life and fosters development.

The care that AI-powered livestock systems enable—converting data into insight and automation into vigilant guardianship—is ultimately what truly has intelligence. With the help of compassionate technology, farming in this new era goes beyond simple work to become a conscientious act of stewardship.

AI-powered livestock feeding and monitoring systems are the epitome of smart agriculture's potential for accuracy, initiative, and output. In addition to increasing yields, farmers may encourage environmental stewardship and animal welfare by utilizing real-time data and sophisticated algorithms.

The barn, driven by data, directed by AI, and grounded in sustainability, is growing as intelligent as the field as we move closer to fully autonomous smart farms.

Chapter 9: AI-Powered Sustainable Agriculture

Overview: The Need for Agriculture to Be Sustainable

In order to feed the world's expanding population and protect natural resources for coming generations, farming must be sustainable. Climate change, soil degradation, water scarcity, and biodiversity loss pose substantial concerns to agriculture. A new era of sustainable agriculture is being ushered in by AI's revolutionary tools, which empower farmers to adopt resource-efficient, commercially viable, and environmentally sound practices. 4.0.

In agriculture, *sustainability is become a critical requirement rather than an option.* The need for food will continue to grow tremendously as the world's population is expected to reach over 9 billion people by 2050. But many ecosystems have already been strained by conventional farming methods, which also severely increase greenhouse gas emissions, deplete soil health, and deplete water supplies.

Producing more food with less resources while reducing environmental effect and preserving social justice and economic viability is the challenge of the future. By encouraging methods that preserve natural resources, increase biodiversity, and guarantee long-term productivity, sustainable agriculture seeks to strike a balance between these frequently conflicting needs.

Sustainability is now more of a need than a choice in agriculture. By 2050, there will be more than 9 billion people on the planet, which will result in an even greater demand for food. However, conventional farming practices have already put a burden on many ecosystems, including significant increases in greenhouse gas emissions, depletion of soil health, and depletion of water supplies.

The challenge of the future is to produce more food with fewer resources while minimizing the impact on the environment, maintaining social fairness, and maintaining economic viability. Sustainable agriculture aims to balance these often incompatible demands by promoting practices that protect natural resources, boost biodiversity, and ensure long-term productivity.

9.1. Outlining AI's Role in Sustainable Farming

A key component of the shift to sustainable agriculture is quickly emerging: artificial intelligence. AI enables farmers to make more intelligent, effective, and ecologically responsible decisions by incorporating sophisticated algorithms, machine learning, and data analytics into farming operations.

Fundamentally, AI aids in the efficient use of resources such as electricity, water, and fertilizers by making sure that inputs are applied precisely where and when they are required, minimizing waste and harm to the environment. AI-driven precision irrigation systems, for instance, use weather forecasts, plant requirements, and soil moisture levels to effectively administer water, avoiding drought stress and overwatering.

By using computer vision and sensor data to identify early indicators of pests, illnesses, or nutrient deficits, AI improves agricultural health monitoring beyond resource management. Early detection enables focused actions, reducing the need for chemicals and protecting biodiversity and beneficial insects.

By suggesting planting dates and crop rotations that preserve soil fertility and lessen erosion, AI also promotes sustainable land use. AI algorithms assist farmers in crop diversification and ecological preservation by evaluating past data and environmental circumstances.

Additionally, AI enables predictive analytics to foresee market patterns and climate consequences, allowing farmers to proactively adjust their operations and lessen their exposure to climate change while maintaining economic viability.

In conclusion, artificial intelligence (AI) is a potent instrument for coordinating environmental stewardship and agricultural output.

It helps create resilient food systems that satisfy present demands without endangering the ability of future generations to flourish by transforming farming from reactive to predictive and from generalist to highly customized.

Long-term ecosystem health, social justice, and economic viability are the main goals of sustainable farming. AI promotes sustainability through:

- Optimizing inputs (pesticides, fertilizer, and water) to cut down on pollution and waste.
- Increasing biodiversity by diversifying crops and using precision planting.
- Reducing climate risks through practice adaptation and weather extreme prediction.
- Enhancing soil health through customized interventions and real-time monitoring.
- Cutting greenhouse gas emissions through resource efficiency.

9.1.1. Diagram: AI-Powered Sustainable Agriculture

AI in Technology	Application in Sustainability
Precision Agriculture	Crop management that is site-specific lowers energy and chemical usage.
Machine Learning	Anticipate insect outbreaks and deficits in soil nutrients to prevent the need for sweeping treatments.
Satellite and Drone Imagery	For focused interventions, keep an eye on crop health, soil erosion, and water consumption.
Robotics & Automation	Reduce soil compaction by conducting focused weeding and harvesting.
AI Powered Forecasting	AI-Powered Forecasting Support agricultural diversification plans and climate-smart planting schedules.

Figure 17: AI-Powered Sustainable Agriculture

9.2. Case Study 1: IBM's Agriculture Watson Decision Platform

IBM's AI Watson Agriculture Technology helps farmers in the US and Brazil use less water and fertilizer by combining weather forecasts, IoT devices, and satellite data.

Results:

- Water use can be decreased by up to 30%.
- A 25% reduction in fertilizer application, which lowers nitrate runoff.
- By anticipating areas that are vulnerable to erosion, soil conservation was enhanced.

9.3. Case Study 2: India's Precision Irrigation and Microsoft AI for Earth

With **AI-Powered Irrigation** scheduling based on soil moisture sensors and meteorological data, **Microsoft's AI for Earth** effort helps Indian farmers.

Impact:

- Effective utilization of water in wheat and rice plantations.
- A 40% reduction in water waste.
- Higher crop yields in unpredictable monsoon seasons.

9.4. Using AI to Monitor and Renew Soil Health

The cornerstone of sustainable agriculture is healthy soil. Strong agricultural growth, improved water retention, carbon storage, and a variety of habitats are all supported by healthy soils. However, global soil degradation brought on by intensive farming methods, excessive chemical use, and climate change is endangering both environmental balance and food security.

With real-time insights and practical suggestions that support long-term soil vitality, artificial intelligence (AI) technologies are transforming how farmers monitor, manage, and rejuvenate soil health.

9.4.1. AI-Powered Soil Monitoring:

These intricate datasets are analysed by machine learning algorithms to produce a thorough soil health profile with a high geographic resolution.

Early identification of indicators of soil deterioration, such as erosion, salinization, or nutrient depletion, is made possible by this ongoing monitoring. Farmers are able to accurately monitor changes over time, allowing for prompt responses that stop irreparable harm.

9.4.2. Precision Soil Management:

Farmers can apply soil amendments, such fertilizers, lime, or organic matter, in a site-specific way with the aid of AI-driven decision support systems for precision soil management. AI algorithms suggest the best kinds, quantities, and timing of inputs based on the specific soil conditions in a given area rather than applying them all at once. This focused strategy minimizes runoff pollution of the environment, cuts expenses, and decreases input waste.

9.4.3. Encouragement of Soil Regeneration Techniques

Regenerative agriculture methods, which naturally repair soil health, are also guided by AI. AI models recommend crop rotations, cover cropping plans, and conservation tillage techniques that increase soil organic matter and enhance structure by evaluating soil data in conjunction with crop performance and weather trends.

AI may, for instance, determine which cover crop species are best suited to fix nitrogen or stop erosion in a particular field, improving biodiversity and nutrient cycling. Additionally, it can increase soil carbon sequestration by managing residues and planting at the right times.

9.4.4. Predicting Trends in Soil Health

AI predicts how soil health will change under various management scenarios and climatic situations by utilizing big data and predictive analytics. Farmers and legislators may identify regions that require immediate repair and implement sustainable land-use strategies thanks to this foresight.

Agriculture can transition to methods that support the soil as a living ecosystem by incorporating AI for soil health monitoring and rejuvenation. AI is a vital enabler of the future of sustainable farming since healthy soils not only maintain productivity but also play a crucial role in reducing climate change and protecting biodiversity.

The foundation of sustainability is healthy soil. AI evaluates in-field sensors and multispectral imagery to determine:

- Soil organic carbon levels;
- Moisture retention capacity;
- Nutrient content and pH fluctuations.

To restore soil fertility, AI models suggest crop rotation, cover crops, and organic amendment programs.

9.5. AI for Pest Control and Biodiversity

Since unregulated pest populations can destroy crops and lower yields, effective pest control is essential for sustainable agriculture. However, conventional approaches that mostly rely on chemical pesticides frequently damage beneficial insects, disturb ecosystems, and fuel the development of resistance. AI-powered pest control provides a more intelligent, well-rounded strategy that safeguards crops and conserves biodiversity.

9.5.1. AI-Assisted Identification and Detection of Pests

AI systems examine photos from cameras, drones, and field sensors using computer vision and machine learning to precisely and early identify and detect pest species. Instead of using broad-spectrum pesticides, this approach allows for specific targeting of interventions by differentiating between beneficial insects and destructive pests.

9.5.2. Modelling Predictive Pest Outbreaks

To anticipate pest outbreaks before they happen, AI models analyse past pest data, meteorological trends, and crop conditions. Because of this foresight, farmers can minimize the usage of pesticides and their negative effects on the environment by implementing preventive measures like habitat management or biological controls.

9.5.3. Optimization of Integrated Pest Management (IPM)

By suggesting customized approaches that include biological, cultural, mechanical, and chemical controls, AI aids integrated pest management. AI assists farmers in making real-time tactical adjustments by continuously evaluating field data and pest dynamics, increasing efficacy while lowering dependency on dangerous chemicals.

9.5.4. AI-Powered Biodiversity

Promotion Biodiversity is essential to sustainable agriculture and robust ecosystems. AI helps by keeping an eye on pollinators, beneficial insect populations, and natural pest predators to make sure their habitats are protected or improved.

AI, for instance, may determine where floral strips or hedgerows that benefit pollinators and pest-repelling natural enemies should be planted.

AI also assists in evaluating the ecological effects of pest management strategies, directing farmers toward methods that preserve or enhance biodiversity on their farms.

Sustainable agriculture may lower chemical inputs, safeguard beneficial species, and promote healthy ecosystems by utilising AI for precision pest management. Long-term agricultural productivity and environmental health depend on striking a balance between crop protection and biodiversity conservation.

Pesticides, which damage ecosystems and beneficial insects, are a major component of traditional pest control. AI makes it possible for:

- Integrated insect Management (IPM) by identifying natural predators and forecasting insect populations.
- Early detection of invasive species by computer vision.
- The targeted use of mechanical control methods or bio-pesticides.

9.10. Prospects for AI-Powered Sustainable Agriculture

The ongoing development and uptake of artificial intelligence technology is closely linked to the future of sustainable agriculture. AI provides strong tools to make agriculture a more resilient, effective, and environmentally friendly system as global issues like population expansion, climate change, and resource scarcity worsen.

9.10.1. Increasing the Farm's Integration of AI

The full agricultural value chain will increasingly be covered by emerging AI applications, ranging from supply chain optimization and market forecasting to crop management and soil health monitoring. AI systems will give farmers immediate, location-specific insights through enhanced sensor technology, real-time data processing, and edge computing, enabling hyper-precise agricultural methods that optimize yields and conserve resources.

9.10.2. Improved Resilience and Climate Adaptation

AI-powered models will advance in their ability to forecast and lessen the effects of illnesses, pests, and extreme weather. This capacity will lessen farmers' susceptibility to climate fluctuation and improve food security by assisting them in proactively adjusting agricultural patterns, irrigation schedules, and pest management techniques.

9.10.3. Democratization and AI Tool Accessibility

Smallholder and resource-poor farmers will have access to AI-powered agriculture platforms as they become more accessible and user-friendly, which will help close the productivity gap and advance equitable growth. AI-enabled advising systems, cloud-based services, and mobile apps will enable farmers everywhere to implement sustainable practices that are suited to their particular circumstances.

9.10.4. Connectivity with Additional Emerging Technologies

AI will more frequently come into contact with blockchain, biotechnology, and robots. AI-guided autonomous farming equipment will further minimize environmental effect and manpower requirements. The creation of robust crop types will be accelerated by genetic analysis and AI-assisted breeding. Blockchain and AI together can improve traceability and transparency in sustainable supply chains, increasing consumer confidence.

9.10.5. Policy and Ethical Aspects to Consider

AI's potential in sustainable agriculture also hinges on resolving moral, societal, and legal issues. To fully utilize AI, it will be essential to protect data privacy, avoid algorithmic biases, and promote inclusive innovation. To develop frameworks that encourage the appropriate application of AI in line with sustainability objectives, policymakers and stakeholders must work together.

Sustainable agriculture driven by AI holds forth the possibility of a time when social well-being, environmental health, and productivity all coexist together. Farmers may provide a really sustainable legacy for future generations by utilizing sophisticated technologies to meet the world's expanding food demand while protecting the planet's natural resources.

9.10.6. Diagram: Obstacles to the Adoption of Sustainable AI

Challenge	Explanation
Data Availability and Quality	The accuracy of AI models for sustainability is limited by scarce or inconsistent data.
Access Inequality	Farmers and smallholders in developing nations might not have access to AI tools.
High Initial Investment	High initial outlay of FundsUpfront expenses for sensors, software, and training are frequently necessary for sustainable AI systems.
Complexity of Ecosystems	Ecosystem Complexity In order to prevent unexpected outcomes, AI models must adjust to local ecological complexity.

Figure 18: Obstacles to the Adoption of Sustainable AI

9.11. Real-World Examples of AI Powered Sustainable Farming

- **Blue River Technology (John Deere):** Using AI-powered "See & Spray" technology, Blue River Technology (John Deere) reduces chemical use by up to 90% by precisely applying herbicides only where necessary. This is an example of AI-powered sustainable farming in action.
- **CropX** is an AI-powered soil sensor platform that recommends irrigation to increase water efficiency and promote drought resistance.
- **Taranis:** Reduces pesticide abuse by using drones and AI analysis to identify agricultural illnesses early.

9.12. Final Thoughts: Using AI to Develop a Sustainable Future

In order to feed a growing population while protecting the environment, *sustainable agriculture becomes increasingly important as the world community deals with more pressing environmental, social, and economic issues*. With its creative approaches to resource optimization, waste reduction, and ecological balance, artificial intelligence is at the vanguard of this revolution.

Previously unthinkable levels of precision and foresight in farming methods are made possible by AI's capacity to interpret large and complicated datasets. AI technologies enable farmers to make timely, well-informed decisions that simultaneously improve productivity and sustainability, from managing pests to monitoring soil health, from optimizing water use to boosting biodiversity.

To fully realize AI's promise, though, *it will need to be carefully integrated with traditional knowledge, accessible to farmers of all sizes, and subject to strict ethical standards that guarantee justice, openness, and privacy*. To develop AI systems that are reliable, flexible, and fair, scientists, legislators, tech developers, and farmers must work together.

In the long run, artificial intelligence (AI) is a potent enabler rather than a cure-all. It is a component of a larger plan to create sustainable food systems that respect social norms and environmental constraints. *Humanity may steer toward a future where farming sustains both people and the environment, guaranteeing wealth for future generations, by adopting AI-driven sustainable agriculture*.

AI is a key component of sustainable agriculture's future since it allows farmers to strike a balance between environmental stewardship and productivity. In the face of climatic uncertainty,

Artificial Intelligence (AI) enhances food security by utilizing real-time data and intelligent decision-making to protect natural resources.

Although the path to sustainable farming is intricate and multidimensional, artificial intelligence (AI) offers a potent ally, reshaping farms, fields, and futures in the direction of a robust, flourishing agricultural ecosystem.

Chapter 10: Case Studies in Smart Farms Worldwide

Overview: Innovations in Smart Farming in the Real World

Smart farms are revolutionizing agriculture worldwide by converting conventional methods into incredibly effective, data-driven businesses. To maximize output, cut waste, and improve sustainability, these farms integrate automation, robots, IoT, AI, and satellite data.

This chapter *explores world-class intelligent farms that represent the state-of-the-art in smart agriculture.* We investigate how technology is changing farming methods, raising yields, and fostering sustainability by looking at a variety of case studies, from large-scale commercial operations to smallholder farms using AI and automation. The practical advantages, difficulties, and lessons discovered by implementing AI-powered systems in many climates, cultures, and crop varieties are demonstrated by these real-world examples.

10.1. Case Study 1: Iron Ox, USA's Robot-Driven Farm

Location: California, USA

Overview: California-based **Iron Ox** is a leader in robotic agriculture, utilizing AI and automation to transform indoor farming. Advanced robotics and machine intelligence are used in their fully autonomous greenhouse to maximize crop growth, minimize resource use, and boost productivity.

Farm Configuration and Technology:

- **Robotic Systems**: Iron Ox uses a fleet of self-governing robots to move, plant, transplant, and harvest plants all across the complex. With the aid of AI-powered sensors and cameras, these robots manoeuvre with accuracy.
- **Hydroponic Environment:** The farm uses hydroponics, which uses up to 90% less water than traditional farming by growing plants in nutrient-rich water rather than soil.
- **AI-Driven Monitoring:** Sensors continuously measure plant health, light, humidity, and nutrient levels. Real-time analysis of this data by AI systems helps to improve growing conditions and identify illnesses early.

Important Innovations:

- **Complete Automation:** Iron Ox's method produces consistent, high-quality production with a significant reduction in human labour.
- **Data-Driven Crop Management:** By using gathered data, machine learning algorithms forecast the most effective growth practices, increasing production and decreasing waste.

- **Sustainability Focus:** Local production and resource efficiency lessen the farm's impact on the environment and supply chain.

Key Innovations Include:

- **Full Automation:** The farm's methodology illustrates how robotics may make farming more scalable, sustainable, and less reliant on manual labour.
- **Data Driven Crop Management:** Iron Ox can produce leafy greens with consistent quality and year-round supply, regardless of external weather conditions.
- **Sustainability Focus:** It provides a model for urban agricultural solutions, enabling communities to have fresh produce closer to their residents.

Obstacles include:

- The high initial capital cost of infrastructure and robots;
- The need for ongoing system maintenance and updates due to technical complexity.
- Consumer education and market acceptability of produce grown by robots.

Future Prospects:

- Developing crop types other than leafy greens.
- Optimizing distribution through the integration of AI with supply chain logistics; expanding the paradigm to additional global cities.

10.2. Case Study 2: Kenyan iCow Climate Smart Farming

Location: Kenya

Overview: Based in Kenya, **iCow** is a ground-breaking mobile platform that provides smallholder farmers with climate-smart agricultural advice powered by artificial intelligence (AI) with an emphasis on crop and livestock management. Through the use of data analytics and mobile technology, iCow assists farmers in enhancing productivity, raising revenue, and adapting to climate variability.

Technology and Platform:

- **Mobile SMS and App-Based Service:** iCow overcomes infrastructure issues in rural areas by sending customized farming advice, reminders, and warnings straight to farmers' mobile phones via SMS and smartphone apps.
- **AI-Powered Advisory**: The platform provides tailored guidance on breeding, feeding, pest management, and planting schedules by utilizing AI to evaluate local meteorological data, animal health, and crop conditions.
- **Data Collection and Feedback**: Farmers provide information on their crops and animals, which aids in the improvement of AI models and recommendations for the future.

Important Innovations:

- **Climate Adaptation**: Farmers can take preventative action by using iCow's early warnings on disease outbreaks, floods, and droughts.
- **Livestock Health Monitoring**: Farmers are reminded

about immunizations, mating cycles, and nutrition management by AI-powered notifications.
- **Inclusive Access:** By making smart farming advice widely available, iCow, which was created for farmers using simple phones, closes the digital gap.

Results and Impact:

- Participating farmers produced more milk and had healthier livestock.
- Higher crop yields as a result of better timing for pest control and planting.
- Increased food security and farmer income in rural areas that are at risk.
- Youth and female farmers are empowered by easily accessible technology.

Difficulties:

- Limited smartphone adoption limits the utilization of full app capabilities.
- Reliance on cell network connectivity, which in isolated locations may not always be dependable.
- To optimize platform benefits, farmers must get ongoing training and interaction.

Future Plans:

- Extension of AI advising services to cover additional livestock and crop species.
- Using weather and satellite data to anticipate the climate more accurately.
- Collaborations with financial institutions to connect

farmers with insurance and loan options.

10.3. Case Study 3: Finca La Anita, Argentina's Precision Viticulture

Location: Argentina's Mendoza

Overview: Using precision agriculture methods to maximize grape output and enhance wine quality, **Finca La Anita** is a premier vineyard in Argentina's Mendoza area. The farm adjusts vineyard management techniques to meet market demands and climatic unpredictability by combining AI, IoT sensors, and data analytics.

Farm Configuration and Technology:

- **Internet of Things Sensor Network**: To keep an eye on conditions at a fine level, temperature probes, microclimate stations, and dispersed soil moisture sensors gather data in real time throughout the vineyard.
- **AI-Driven Analytics:** To optimize fertilization, pest management, and irrigation schedules, machine learning models evaluate sensor data in conjunction with weather forecasts.
- **Drones and Imaging**: To evaluate vine health, identify illnesses, and track growth stages, aerial drones fitted with multispectral cameras take high-resolution pictures.

Important innovations include:

- **Precision Irrigation**, which maximizes grape quality while conserving resources by applying water in variable amounts according to plant and soil requirements
- **Disease Management and Prediction**: AI systems can detect early symptoms of fungal infections, such as powdery mildew, allowing for more focused treatments and less chemical usage.

- **Yield Forecasting**: To help with supply chain planning, data-driven models forecast harvest volumes and grape quality weeks in advance.

Results and Effects:

- Better grape consistency and quality, which results in more expensive wines.
- Considerable water conservation in an area vulnerable to drought stress.
- Precise application of pesticides results in less usage, supporting environmental sustainability.
- Improved capacity to use adaptive management in response to climate unpredictability.

Obstacles include:

- The upfront expenses and training needed for traditional vineyard workers to incorporate technology.
- The difficulty of integrating data from many sources and sensor kinds.
- Applying precise scaling methods to various vineyard topographies.

Prospects for the Future:

- Blockchain integration for wine traceability and provenance.
- The creation of AI models customized for various terrors and grape varieties.
- Increased automation of vineyard operations like harvesting and trimming.

10.4. Case Study 4: Xarvio Digital Farming, Germany's Autonomous Tractors

Where: Germany

Overview: Using AI-driven software and autonomous tractor technology, Bayer's **Xarvio Digital Farming** is leading the way in precision agriculture in Germany and maximizes crop yields. The platform from Xarvio gives farmers automated equipment and data-driven insights to increase productivity, cut expenses, and promote sustainability.

Farm Configuration and Technology:

- **Self-Driving Tractors** with GPS, sensors, and artificial intelligence (AI) are being used for planting, spraying, and harvesting by Xarvio in collaboration with tractor manufacturers. Following accurate field maps, these devices function with little assistance from humans.
- **Digital Farming Platform**: To create variable rate recommendations for irrigation, fertilization, and pesticide application, the Xarvio FIELD MANAGER software examines weather information, satellite imagery, and field-level data.
- **Real-Time Monitoring:** Continuous data feedback from sensors on tractors and in fields enables real-time changes and resource optimization.

Important Innovations:

- **Precision Application**: By ensuring that inputs like insecticides and fertilizers are only applied where necessary, variable rate technology lowers waste and its negative effects on the environment.

- **Automated Field Operations:** Farmers can concentrate on strategic planning and decision-making with the help of autonomous tractors, which also improve operational efficiency.
- **Integration with Digital Advisory**: AI-generated suggestions tailored to farmers' fields, crops, and regional circumstances are provided.

Results and Impact:

- Precise management leads to higher crop yields and lower input costs.
- A smaller carbon footprint as a result of less idle machinery and better resource use.
- Increased worker safety and productivity with reduced manual tractor operation.
- Increased capacity to adjust to shifting climatic circumstances and weather variability.

Challenges:

- Expensive initial outlay for digital infrastructure and driverless machinery.
- Reliable network access is required in order to facilitate real-time data transfer.
- Safety and regulatory issues surrounding the use of driverless vehicles in rural regions.

Future Plans:

- Increasing the capacity of autonomous machinery to do additional agricultural duties.

- Better AI models that use larger datasets for even more precise administration.
- Working together with governmental organizations to create safety guidelines and standards.

10.5. Case Study 5: Nigeria's Zenvus Smart Farm

Where: Nigeria

Overview: Using IoT sensors and AI-powered data analytics, **Zenvus** is a cutting-edge **Nigerian Agritech firm** that is transforming smart farming. Particularly at small to medium-sized farms, which are prevalent in Nigeria and West Africa, Zenvus helps farmers boost productivity and sustainability by providing accurate soil and crop health monitoring and management through the use of smart sensors on farms.

Farm Configuration and Technology:

- **IoT Soil Sensors**: Zenvus provides farmers with useful information about soil health by deploying reasonably priced sensors that assess soil temperature, moisture content, pH, and nutrient levels in real-time.
- **AI Data Analytics:** Using AI algorithms, data gathered from the sensors is examined to produce plot-specific suggestions for fertilizer application, irrigation timing, and pest control.
- **Mobile Platform**: Even in areas with inadequate physical infrastructure, farmers may manage their farms remotely by using a mobile app to access their farm data and receive notifications.

Important Innovations:

- **Affordably Precision Agriculture:** Zenvus provides smallholder farmers with inexpensive sensor kits to overcome the financial obstacle.
- **Localized Recommendations**: To offer context-specific

guidance, AI models are trained using local soil and climatic data.

- **Data-Driven Decision Support**: By providing farmers with timely insights, the platform increases agricultural yields and input efficiency.

Results and Effects:

- Shown improvements in crop yields and the efficiency of input utilization for farmers utilizing Zenvus technology.
- Better monitoring of soil health results in more environmentally friendly farming methods and less environmental deterioration.
- Improved farmer empowerment and knowledge thanks to mobile connectivity and data literacy.
- Assistance with dependable farm data for government and agricultural extension initiatives.

Challenges include:

- In certain rural locations, there is limited smartphone penetration and internet availability.
- To optimize the deployment of technology, farmers require continuous technical assistance and instruction.
- Expanding the solutions' reach to include more farmers in various agro-ecological zones.

Future Plans:

- Combining satellite data and weather forecasting for more thorough agricultural management.
- Development of AI-powered picture analysis for crop disease identification.

- Collaborations with financial institutions to provide insurance and financing based on farm profiles derived from data.

10.6. Case Study 6: New Jersey, USA's AeroFarms Vertical Farming

Where: Newark, New Jersey, United States

Overview: AeroFarms, a global leader in **Vertical Farming** with its headquarters located in New Jersey, uses aeroponics and artificial intelligence (AI)-driven environmental control systems to cultivate herbs and leafy greens indoors in urban settings. With this strategy, fresh produce is delivered near consumers all year round while maximizing space efficiency and minimizing resource consumption.

Farm Configuration and Technology:

- **Aeroponic Growing System:** Unlike traditional farming, this method uses up to 95% less water because plants grow without soil, with roots hanging in the air and misted with nutrient-rich fluids.
- **AI Environmental Controls:** Sensors keep an eye on temperature, light, humidity, and nutrient levels. For optimal plant development, AI systems continuously optimize these settings.
- **Data Analytics**: In order to improve crop yields and quality, AeroFarms gathers a great deal of data on plant growth trends.

Important Innovations:

- **Space-Efficient Vertical Layers**: In urban areas with limited land, vertical farming increases output per square foot by stacking numerous growth layers.
- **Sustainable Resource Use:** By recycling nutrients and water, the system drastically lowers waste and its negative effects on the environment.

- **Year-Round Production:** Seasonality and weather-related hazards are eliminated by a controlled indoor environment.

Results and Effects:

- Reliable, superior product with quicker growth cycles than crops cultivated in fields.
- A decrease in food miles and the transportation sector's carbon footprint.
- Greater food security in cities through localizing the production of fresh crops.
- Good social impact by generating jobs in the technology and urban agricultural industries.

Obstacles include:

- Expensive start-up and maintenance costs for vertical farm infrastructure.
- Energy use for climate control and artificial lighting, however lessened by the use of renewable energy.
- Market awareness and consumer acceptance of produce grown vertically.

Future Prospects:

- Increasing the number of crop varieties that include fruits and vegetables in addition to leafy greens.
- Integration with intelligent logistics systems to improve supply chain administration.
- Making use of machine learning to improve operational efficiency and predictive maintenance.

10.6.1. Diagram: Takeaways and Common Themes

Theme	Insights
Data Integration Key	To increase AI accuracy, successful farms integrate data from satellites, IoT, weather, and soil.
Scalability Across Farm Sizes	AI is flexible enough to work in a variety of settings and scales, from industrial farms (Iron Ox) to smallholder platforms (iCow).
Labour Transformation	Although automation eliminates manual labour, controlling and monitoring AI systems calls for new talents.
Sustainability Focus	The advantages of smart farms are similar in terms of water, energy, and chemical savings.
Localised Solutions Matter	Adoption and impact are increased when AI solutions are tailored to local crops, climate, and farmer needs.

Figure 19: Takeaways and Common Themes

10.7. Smart Farms' Future Directions

- **AI-Human Hybrid Farming Models:** AI helps farmers while maintaining customs and knowledge.
- **AI-Enabled Supply Chain Integration**: To cut waste, farms use AI to connect directly with markets and logistics.
- **Farm Data Marketplaces**: In exchange for insights, farmers exchange anonymised data to enhance AI models.
- **Global Smart Farm Networks**: Farms all across the world can benchmark, learn, and innovate thanks to collaborative AI ecosystems.

10.8. Final Thoughts: Gaining Knowledge from the Frontlines

Globally, smart farms provide useful models for agriculture's future. These farms show how technology can boost resilience, sustainability, and productivity by adopting AI-driven innovation. These models will be essential in feeding a burgeoning population and safeguarding the environment as they proliferate and develop.

Chapter 11: Difficulties, Restrictions, and Moral Issues

Overview: Handling the Difficulties of AI in Farming

Even though AI has the potential to revolutionize agriculture, adoption of this technology is fraught with difficulties, ethical quandaries, and technical constraints. To ensure AI's responsible, egalitarian, and sustainable integration into farming systems around the world, it is imperative to comprehend these factors.

11.1. Technical Difficulties

a. AI and Carbon Farming

Artificial intelligence (AI) systems will measure the amount of carbon sequestered by plants and soils, advising farmers on methods that optimize carbon storage and maybe creating new markets for carbon credits.

Availability and Quality of Data

- **Issue:** For AI models to be accurate, enormous volumes of high-quality, labelled data are needed. A lot of agricultural areas, particularly in developing nations, struggle with insufficient or irregular data gathering.
- **Impact:** Inaccurate forecasts and a decline in farmer confidence in AI solutions are caused by poor data.
- **Example:** Soil nutrient maps may be imprecise or out-of-date, leading to incorrect fertilizer recommendations.

a. Limitations in Infrastructure

- **Issue:** AI frequently requires dependable power, internet access, and cloud computing capabilities—all of which are scarce in rural regions.
- **Impact:** Adoption of AI tools by smallholder farmers may encounter obstacles.
- **Example:** Areas with poor cellphone coverage might not be able to support real-time drone observation.

a. Integration and Interoperability

- **Issue:** Incompatible data formats or standards may be used by various AI tools and IoT devices.

- **Impact:** Holistic farm management is made more difficult by fragmented data ecosystems.
- **Fix:** For smooth integration, open platforms and industry standards are required.

11.2. Social and Economic Restrictions

a. **Expensive starting costs**

- **Problem:** It can be prohibitively expensive to spend upfront in sensors, AI systems, and training.
- **Repercussion**: If advantages are modest or delayed, small-scale farmers run the risk of being excluded or incurring debt.
- **Mitigation:** Microfinance, cooperative methods, and subsidies can all aid in expanding access.

a. **Skills Gap and Digital Literacy**

- **Difficulty**: A lot of farmers are not proficient in using sophisticated technology or interpreting AI information.
- **Impact:** AI tools that are misused or underutilized become less effective.
- **Fix:** User-friendly interfaces and training courses are crucial.

a. **Issues with Job Displacement**

- **Problem:** AI and automation may lessen the need for conventional farm labour.
- **Reaction:** Policies ought to support transition plans and labour reskilling.

11.3. Moral Aspects

a. **Data Ownership and Privacy**

- **Issue:** *Who is the owner of farm data that AI systems gather? How is it shared, stored, or made money off of?*
- **Danger:** Farmers run the danger of prejudice or exploitation if they lose control over sensitive data.
- **Best Practice**: Consent from farmers and transparent data policies are essential.

a. **AI Models' Bias and Fairness**

- **Problem:** AI that has been educated on data from developed areas might not function effectively in other situations, producing unfair results.
- **Example:** AI for pest identification that was taught on temperate crops may not work well in tropical agriculture.
- **Take Action:** Context-aware models and inclusive datasets are required.

a. **Environmental Impact**

- **Worry**: Using more high-tech equipment could result in energy usage and electronic waste.
- **Balance:** AI should minimize its own carbon impact while optimizing resource utilization.

11.4. Governance and Regulation Difficulties

- *There is uncertainty around liability, standards, and compliance because to the absence of AI-specific agriculture rules.*
- *Concerns regarding intellectual property and sovereignty are brought up by cross-border data flows.*
- *To create frameworks guaranteeing safety, openness, and fair access, governments and business must cooperate together.*

11.5. Case Study: Moral Conundrums in AI-Powered Pest Management

AI-guided drones that sprayed pesticides only where pests were identified were introduced by a start-up. However, the system was unable to detect helpful insects, which resulted in an ecological imbalance and negative reactions from farmers.

Instruction: Before being implemented, AI solutions must undergo extensive testing for their effects on society and the environment.

11.5.1. Description of Strategies for Responsible AI Adoption

Strategy	Description
Participatory Design	Engage local communities and farmers in the creation of AI tools through participatory design.
Transparency & Explainability	Make sure users can comprehend and challenge AI judgments.
Data Sovereignty	Put in place systems that allow farmers to manage their data.
Sustainability Metrix	Include social and environmental metrics in assessments of AI's performance.
Ethical Auditing	Frequent evaluations of AI systems' influence, fairness, and bias.

Figure 20: Description of Strategies for Responsible AI Adoption

11.6. Outlook for the Future

- The creation of inexpensive offline AI solutions to fill up connectivity gaps.
- The emergence of agriculturally specific AI ethics frameworks.
- More public-private collaborations to make AI more accessible to everybody.
- The development of "explainable AI" in AI to increase farmer trust.

In summary: Innovation and Responsibility in Balance

AI in agriculture holds great promise, but responsible adoption necessitates navigating challenging ethical, social, and technical environments. Stakeholders can guarantee AI improves farming in a sustainable, equitable, and transparent manner by proactively tackling these issues, contributing to the development of a future in which technology genuinely empowers all farmers.

Chapter 12: Developing Resilient Agricultural Systems: The Path Ahead

Overview: Agriculture's Need for Resilience

Climate change, population increase, resource scarcity, and geopolitical instability present agriculture with hitherto unheard-of difficulties. Global food security depends on the development of resilient agricultural systems that can adjust to shocks and pressures while retaining productivity. These resilient systems of the future will be designed, managed, and maintained in large part by AI and digital technology.

12.1. Agricultural Resilience: What Is It?

The ability of farming systems to:

- Resist and bounce back from environmental stressors including droughts, floods, and pest outbreaks is known as *Agricultural Resilience.*
- Proactively adjust to shifting socioeconomic and climatic situations; as required, switch to new crops or techniques to maintain ecosystems and livelihoods.

12.2. AI as a Resilience Catalyst

Resilience Aspect	AI Contribution
Early warning and Risk Assessment	AI models provide prompt mitigation by forecasting disease outbreaks, pest invasions, and weather extremes.
Diversification and Crop Selection	AI suggests robust crop varieties and rotations by analysing market, soil, and climatic data.
Resource Optimisation	Precision farming enabled by AI reduces susceptibility by optimizing the use of energy, water, and nutrients.
Supply Chain Adaptability	Even in the face of disruptions, AI enables flexible logistics and market access.

Figure 21: AI as a Resilience Catalyst

12.3. Case Study 3: Climate Resilience in India Driven by AI

The Indian Council of Agricultural Research (ICAR) advises farmers on the following topics:

- Using AI-driven climate models and local farm data:
- Choosing drought-resistant crop varieties;
- Managing soil moisture;

Impact:

- A 20% decrease in crop failures
- Smallholder farmers' increased financial stability and
- Increased use of climate-smart methods

12.4. Using AI to Improve Water and Soil Resilience

Soil and water are essential to agriculture. Even the most sophisticated farming techniques cannot generate sustainable crops without good soil and enough water. Because of the burden that climate change, misuse, and bad management methods have placed on these resources, contemporary agriculture has made resilience a primary concern. An increasingly potent ally in the monitoring, control, and restoration of the delicate equilibrium of soil and water systems is artificial intelligence.

1. Water Resilience with AI

Global food production is under threat from extreme weather events, water scarcity, and erratic rainfall patterns. AI can help with these issues by:

a. Intelligent Watering Systems

- AI-powered irrigation systems optimize watering schedules using real-time sensor data, weather predictions, and soil moisture measurements.
- **Example:** Netafim uses AI and IoT devices to pinpoint the precise quantity of water required for each crop, cutting waste and increasing yields.
- **Advantage:** Compared to conventional irrigation, farmers can save anywhere from 30% to 50% on water use.

a. Modelling Predictive Water Demand

During droughts or peak seasons, proactive resource distribution is made possible by machine learning models that can predict water demand weeks or months in advance.

Example: AI systems in the Central Valley of California forecast seasonal water requirements and advise decision-makers on water restrictions.

a. Monitoring Water Quality

Artificial intelligence (AI)-powered picture identification and spectroscopic techniques can identify hazardous algal blooms, salt levels, and chemical contaminants in irrigation water.

As an illustration, the World Bank's Smart Water Project in India employs artificial intelligence (AI) to evaluate satellite imagery in order to detect water contamination early.

1. AI for Resilient Soils

A global crisis, soil deterioration is brought on by chemical contamination, nutrient depletion, and erosion. AI can support soil health monitoring and restoration by:

a. Monitoring and Soil Mapping

High-resolution soil maps displaying nutrient levels, pH balance, organic matter content, and moisture retention capacity can be produced by drones and satellites fitted with artificial intelligence algorithms.

- As an illustration, SoilOptix creates maps that are eight million times more detailed than those produced by conventional soil tests using AI and gamma-ray sensors.

a. **Forecasting and Stopping Soil Degradation**

To find areas that are prone to erosion before degradation happens, machine learning can integrate topographical, rainfall, and land-use data.

- As an illustration, Kenya uses AI-driven erosion models to direct the planting of cover crops and terracing in order to protect topsoil.

a. **Fertilizer Optimization**

AI systems combine crop growth trends and soil health data to suggest accurate fertilizer applications, limiting overuse and nutrient runoff into streams.

1. **Systems of Integrated Water-Soil Resilience**

Integrated water-soil management platforms that integrate AI, IoT, and remote sensing are the way of the future:

- AI could simultaneously track weather forecasts, soil moisture, and nutrient availability, modifying fertilization and irrigation programs in real time.
- Closed-loop farming, which continuously optimizes soil and water inputs for optimal sustainability, is made possible by such technologies.
    1. **Case Study: Australia's AI-Powered Water and Soil Conservation**

Farmers in Australia's drought-prone areas employ an AI system that:

1. Compiles data from soil sensors and satellite pictures.
2. Executes forecasting models for crop water stress and moisture retention.
3. Provides daily advice on soil cover crops, irrigation schedules, and erosion prevention techniques.

Within three years, there was a discernible increase in soil organic matter and a 40% reduction in water usage.

1. **Prospects for the Future**

- **AI-Enabled Bioengineering**: creating crops with water-efficient root systems.
- **Autonomous Soil Regeneration Bots:** Tiny AI-controlled devices that spread organic compost, plant cover crops, and patch erosion channels.
- **Global Soil-Water Resilience Networks:** These shared AI platforms give farmers all across the world real-time access to best practices and predictive models.
    1. **Key Takeaway:**

AI excels at transforming large, intricate environmental data into site-specific, actionable plans that protect soil and water. These kinds of technologies will be necessary for resilient agriculture as climatic pressures increase; they won't be an option.

12.5. AI-Powered Agroforestry and Diversification

Monocultures have long been used in agriculture to increase efficiency, but this strategy exposes farms to pests, illnesses, and market fluctuations. By incorporating trees, bushes, and a variety of crops into farming systems, agroforestry provides a sustainable substitute that boosts biodiversity, strengthens soil, and stabilizes farm profits. Agroforestry and diversification plans may be planned, tracked, and optimized with previously unheard-of accuracy thanks to artificial intelligence.

12.5.1. **Agroforestry's Potential in the AI Era**

Agroforestry is the process of creating intricate, mutually beneficial ecosystems rather than merely planting trees next to crops. AI makes possible:

- Finding the best plant species combinations for resilience and yield is known as data-driven planning.
- Predicting shade, windbreak effects, and soil moisture retention from tree canopies is known as microclimate modelling.
- Biodiversity tracking: keeping an eye on wildlife, pest predators, and pollinators with drones and computer vision.

1. **Agroforestry AI Applications**

a. Selection and Positioning of Species

To suggest the ideal combination of crops, trees, and livestock, AI systems can examine soil profiles, rainfall patterns, market trends, and the potential for carbon sequestration.

- As an illustration, CIFOR-ICRAF plans multi-layered farming systems in Africa by utilizing AI-powered decision-support tools that balance ecological advantages with financial gains.

a. Managing Pests and Diseases in Various Systems

The dynamics of pests are complicated on varied farms. AI-powered image identification and predictive analytics can spot outbreaks early, even in mixed-species plots.

- **Advantage:** Promotes natural insect management and lessens the need for pesticides.

a. Modelling Climate Adaptation

Planting patterns that optimize resilience are guided by machine learning models that mimic the responses of diverse agroforestry systems to climate extremes.

- For instance, AI in the Deccan Plateau of India forecasts how tree cover will lessen heat stress for plants that grow cocoa and coffee.

1. Using AI to Diversify Agriculture Beyond Trees

Integrating several crop rotations for soil fertility and pest resistance is another aspect of diversification.

- Including livestock and aquaculture in agricultural systems.
- AI market forecasting-guided high-value niche crops.
- AI systems are able to model profitability situations and suggest diversification plans based on climatic projections and market demand.

1. **Systems of Integrated Monitoring**

AI can track the growth rates of various species using data from satellites, drones, and Internet of Things devices.

- Identify the rivalry between crops and trees for nutrients.
- Projected yields for cash crops, fruit, and timber in mixed systems.
- Farmers can adjust crop densities, harvest schedules, and resource allocation with the aid of these findings.
    1. **Case Study: Ghanaian Cocoa Agroforestry Assisted by AI**

In Ghana, AI systems incorporate satellite photos, weather data, and soil maps to benefit cocoa farmers:

1. Select shade trees that complement one another to increase biodiversity and cocoa output.
2. Use microclimate data to forecast cocoa quality.
3. Plan your crop to maximize market values.

Outcome: Farmers report a 15% increase in crops and improved long-term soil health.

1. **Prospects for the Future**

- **Digital Twin Farms**: AI models that simulate agroforestry systems to test planting configurations prior to actual deployment.
- **Artificial Intelligence Carbon Credit Platforms**: These platforms measure and validate carbon sequestration from trees automatically in order to produce revenue through carbon markets.

- **Autonomous Agroforestry Robots:** These machines can plant, prune, and keep an eye on tree-crop systems with little assistance from humans.

Key Takeaway: AI makes diversity and agroforestry's complexity an asset rather than a problem. Farmers can create resilient, lucrative, and climate-friendly agricultural landscapes by fusing ecological knowledge and predictive analytics.

12.6. AI-Powered Social Resilience

People are just as important to agricultural resilience as crops, soils, and water. The ability of farming communities to adjust, bounce back, and prosper in the face of shocks like market volatility, climate change, technical advancements, and socio-political unrest is known as social resilience. AI is becoming a disruptive force that can improve collaboration, increase access to information, and facilitate more equitable decision-making, all of which can strengthen the social fabric of agricultural systems.

1. **Recognizing Agriculture's Social Resilience**

Adaptive capacity, or the ability to modify farming methods in response to change, is one aspect of social resilience.

- **Community Networks:** Social ties that exchange information, resources, and assistance.
- **Institutional Trust**: Belief in institutions, partnerships, and regulations.

Ensuring that underrepresented groups have equitable access to resources and decision-making is known as *Inclusivity*. These components can be combined with AI to create community-driven, digitally empowered agricultural ecosystems.

1. **AI-Powered Tools to Boost Social Resilience**

a. **Knowledge platforms powered by AI**

Agricultural knowledge is now available in local languages and customized to particular farm situations thanks to AI-powered chatbots, translation tools, and advisory systems.

- For instance, PlantVillage Nuru diagnoses plant problems for smallholder farmers using AI picture recognition and offers prompt, targeted guidance.

a. **Community Risk Predictive Alerts**

To warn communities of potential dangers, machine learning can examine market swings, pest migration, and weather patterns.

- **Advantage:** Farmers can work together to minimize harm by coordinating pest treatment or planting.

a. **AI in Market and Cooperative Coordination**

AI systems are able to:

- Connect buyers and small-scale producers.
- Forecast crop demand in regional and local markets.
- Reduce post-harvest losses and transportation expenses by streamlining group logistics.

a. **Inclusion With AI**

AI can detect resource access disparities between male and female farmers by evaluating gender-disaggregated data, guaranteeing that underprivileged populations receive inputs, financing, and training.

1. **AI-Enabled Participatory Decision-Making**

AI can help with online community consultations by summarizing a lot of feedback using natural language processing.

- Sentiment analysis to determine the worries of the community.
- Tools for decision-making that strike a balance between immediate need and long-term viability.

1. **Case Study: Kenyan Farmer Cooperatives with AI Support**

Farmer cooperatives in Kenya are able to:

1. Forecast seasonal yields across member farms thanks to AI technologies coupled with mobile apps.
2. Work out better group prices with purchasers.
3. Determine which participants might require emergency assistance or training.

As a result, revenues increased by 20%, and solidarity increased during crop failures caused by climate change.

1. **Prospects for the Future**

- **AI-Powered Rural Education Networks:** Using flexible e-learning platforms, these networks provide distant communities with cutting-edge instruction in business and farming.
- **Community Digital Twins**: Before putting various farming practices into practice, they can simulate their socioeconomic effects.
- **AI for Social Equity Mapping**: Ensuring equitable allocation of agricultural subsidies and funds for climate adaption.

The main conclusion is that AI-powered social resilience makes sure that the use of technology in agriculture doesn't exacerbate inequality but rather improves community relationships, encourages inclusivity, and permits shared prosperity in the face of adversity.

Diagram: AI's Role in Building Resilient Farms

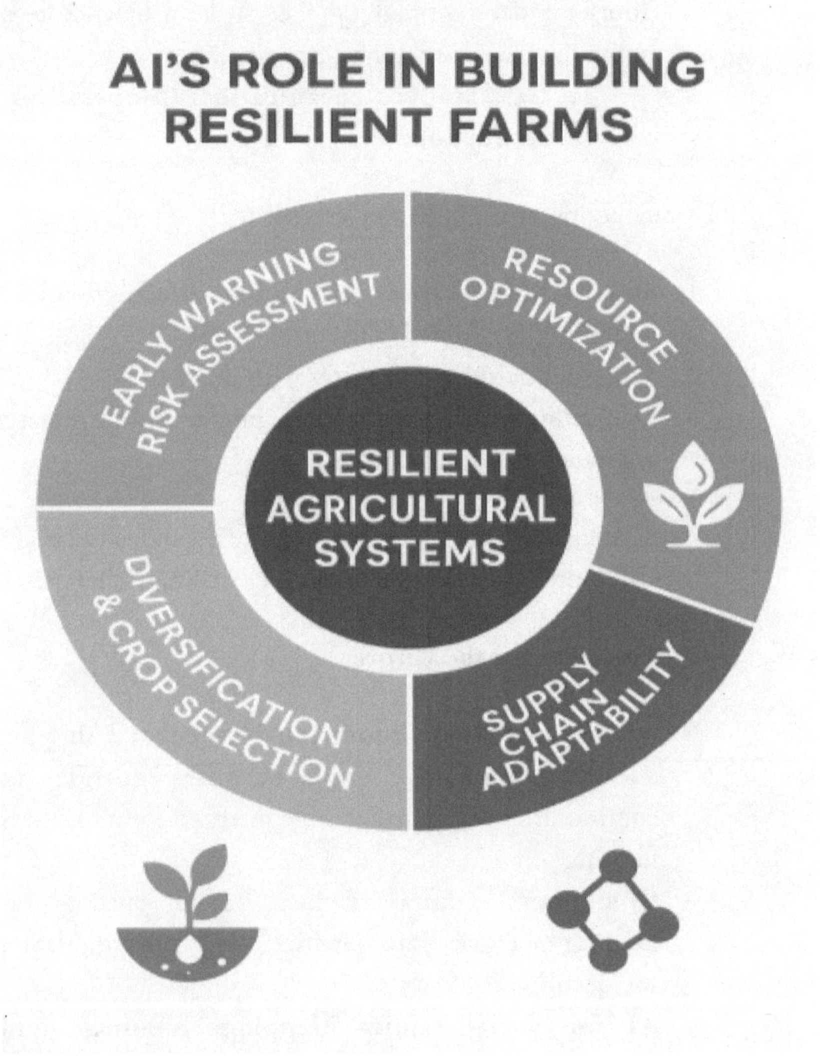

Figure 22: AI's Role in Building Resilient Farms

Diagram: New Technologies Improving Resilience

Technology	Role in Resilience
Blockchain	Blockchain increases supply chain confidence by ensuring traceability, secure transactions, and transparency.
Edge Computing	AI processing on farms is made possible by edge computing, which eliminates the need for erratic internet connectivity.
Synthetic Biology & AI	AI helps create crop types that are more tolerant of stress and climate change.
Swarm Robotics	Targeted pest control and soil management are carried out with the least amount of disturbance by coordinated robot fleets.

Figure 23: New Technologies Improving Resilience

12.7. Difficulties in Developing AI-Powered Resilient Systems

While AI has the potential to transform agricultural resilience, its real-world deployment is frequently far from clear. The effective implementation and long-term viability of AI-powered resilient systems in agriculture may be impeded by a number of interconnected technical, financial, and social issues.

1. **Problems with Data Scarcity and Quality**

Large, high-quality datasets are essential for AI systems to function, but in many agricultural areas, these datasets are infrequent, out-of-date, or inconsistent:

- **Disjointed Data Sources:** Weather data, soil measurements, and farm records are frequently kept in disparate systems.
- **Bias and Incompleteness**: Models that don't generalize effectively are often the result of smallholder farms in developing regions being underrepresented in datasets.
- **Sensor Reliability:** Inaccurate data from malfunctioning or incorrectly calibrated IoT sensors can impair system performance.

Example: Because rainfall data was gathered from far weather stations rather than on-site sensors, an AI-driven irrigation optimization platform in East Africa performed poorly and produced recommendations that were inconsistent.

1. **Expensive Upfront Expenses And Infrastructure**

Constraints

Creating and implementing AI-powered resilience technologies necessitates a large hardware, software, and networking investment.

- **Hardware Costs**: For smallholder farmers, autonomous equipment, drones, and precision sensors may be prohibitively expensive.
- **Connectivity Gaps**: The dependable internet access required for cloud-based analytics and real-time AI model updates is lacking in many rural regions.
- **Maintenance Difficulties**: To maintain and debug AI systems in the field, specialized technical skills are needed.

1. **Adaptability and Robustness of the Model**

Because soil types, climatic patterns, and pest pressures vary greatly between areas and seasons, agricultural ecosystems are extremely varied:

- **Over-fitting Risks**: Models that have been trained in one area may not work in another.
- **Climate Change Uncertainty**: Weather patterns can change quickly, making historical data less accurate.
- **Adaptive Learning Needs:** Although resource-intensive, ongoing retraining is crucial.

For instance: Unexpected changes in insect migration associated with climatic anomalies required an annual recalibration of a pest prediction AI in South Asia.

1. **Social, Legal, And Ethical Obstacles**

Concerns raised by the use of AI systems may impede acceptance or spark opposition.

- **Data Ownership and Privacy:** Without explicit protections, farmers could be hesitant to divulge financial or yield-related sensitive information.
- **Trust Deficit:** Underuse of AI technologies may result from scepticism about "machine-made" recommendations.
- **Regulatory Obstacles**: Developers and investors face legal uncertainties due to the absence of defined frameworks for AI in agriculture.

1. **Problems with Integration and Interoperability**

Agricultural technology ecosystems are frequently dispersed, with several manufacturers providing incompatible proprietary solutions.

- **Closed Architectures:** Certain AI systems are made to work exclusively with particular hardware manufacturers.
- **Integration Costs:** It can be costly and technically challenging to connect AI models with legacy farm management systems.

1. **Issues with Long-Term Sustainability**

AI-powered solutions need to be long-term profitable and functional.

- **Dependency Risks:** Farmers can get dependent on AI subscription services, which could be discontinued or see price increases.
- **Energy Demands**: Sustainability objectives may clash with the high processing demands of model training and inference.

- **Skill Gaps**: Local ability to administer these systems declines in the absence of ongoing training initiatives.

1. **Crucial Knowledge**

The path to AI-powered agricultural resilience involves addressing ingrained problems with infrastructure, trust, adaptability, and inclusion rather than merely creating stronger algorithms. Partnerships between humans and AI that emphasize context-specific solutions, shared data ownership, and long-term capacity building will be essential for sustainable success.

12.8. Institutional and Policy Assistance for Resilience

It takes strong institutions and progressive policies that provide long-term stability, fair access, and flexibility in the face of new challenges to build resilient agricultural systems. Using technology alone is not enough. Although AI can increase resilience, these innovations run the risk of becoming disjointed solutions that fall short of their full potential in the absence of institutional and policy scaffolding.

1. Building Institutional Strength

Institutions that can foresee, adjust, and react to disruptions—whether brought on by pests, market shocks, or climate variability—are the first steps toward resilience:

- **Research and Innovation Hubs:** Hubs for Research and Innovation Create agricultural innovation hubs that combine field testing, local farming expertise, and AI research. AI-driven resilience solutions like pest identification, soil health monitoring, and climate forecasting ought to be developed in these hubs.
- **Extension Services 2.0:** Utilize AI-powered platforms to enhance conventional agricultural extension services. This includes real-time notifications for farmers in remote areas, crop diagnostics on mobile devices, and virtual advising services.
- **Public-Private Partnerships (PPPs)**: To speed up the development of AI tools for resilience, PPPs encourage cooperation between governments, academic institutions, AI start-ups, and agro-industrial stakeholders.

Example: The Agriculture and Food Authority in Kenya collaborates with AI-powered climate forecasting systems to provide more than 2 million smallholder farmers with seasonal planting advice by SMS.

1. **Resilience Policy Frameworks**

Encouraging policies that promote innovation while guaranteeing sustainability, equity, and openness must serve as the foundation for institutional support:

- **Data Governance Policies:** To foster confidence between farmers, AI providers, and governmental organizations, clear rules regarding the ownership, privacy, and sharing of agricultural data are crucial.
- **Climate-Smart Subsidies**: To ensure affordability for smallholders, redirect subsidies toward AI-enabled climate adaption products like predictive pest management or precision irrigation systems.
- **Frameworks for Risk Management**: Create guidelines for AI-powered early warning systems and include them into national strategies for disaster preparedness.

Example: AI-driven satellite data is being used to improve India's *Pradhan Mantri Fasal Bima Yojana* (PMFBY) crop insurance program, allowing for quicker damage assessments and pay-out processing during droughts and floods.

1. **Including Artificial Intelligence in National Agriculture Plans**

Instead of being viewed as an add-on, AI for resilience should be included into long-term agricultural strategies:

- Incorporate AI-powered climate modelling into national strategies for food security.
- Encourage digital literacy initiatives for cooperatives and farmers to guarantee fair access to the advantages of AI.
- Provide incentives for locally adaptable, open-source AI solutions that don't require expensive licensing.

1. **Global Collaboration and Harmonization of Policies**

Cross-border cooperation is frequently necessary for resilience:

- **Regional AI Data Pools:** To enhance prediction models, nearby nations can exchange datasets on crop diseases, soil conditions, and climate.
- **Trade Policy Alignment:** Prevent obstacles to market access by ensuring AI-enabled agricultural processes and products adhere to international trade norms.
- **Joint Funding Mechanisms**: Combine funds for extensive AI-powered resilience initiatives in common ecosystems, including river basins or areas vulnerable to drought.

Example: A common AI-based locust surveillance and response system may be implemented by the Southern African Development Community (SADC), which would increase coverage and speed of response while lowering costs.

1. **Governance for Agriculture's Ethical AI Use**

Policies must guarantee that AI is used ethically, without worsening environmental damage or inequity:

- Require AI technologies to undergo bias audits in order

to avoid biased suggestions that affect underrepresented farming communities.

- Demand environmental impact analyses for extensive agricultural treatments powered by AI.
- Establish review boards with a variety of stakeholders, such as farmers, technologists, legislators, and environmental experts.

12.9. Future Vision: Smart Ecosystems with Resilient Farms

The farm of the future will be an intelligent ecosystem that combines nature-based solutions with AI-driven sensors, robots, and analytics. In order to provide food security even in the face of growing uncertainty, these farms will retain biodiversity, optimize resource flows, and react dynamically to environmental cues.

By 2035, self-learning agricultural ecosystems—networks where farmers, supply chains, and policymakers exchange real-time insights—will start to appear in nations that incorporate AI into their institutional frameworks and policy roadmaps. These networks will allow for a level of agility that is unmatched by current systems. AI intelligence and effective governance will enable resilience to become proactive and adaptable rather than reactive.

In summary: Toward an Agricultural Future That Is Resilient

In a time of societal change and climate instability, creating resilient agricultural systems is not a choice—it is a necessity for life. AI is a potent facilitator, providing the resources and knowledge required to turn farms into resilient, adaptable, and sustainable businesses that will feed the globe for many years to come.

Table of Figures

Bibliography

1. Sirisha Potluri & Suneeta Satpathy; *AI in Agriculture for Sustainable and Economic Management,* Routledge, 2024
2. Kativa Pandey et al.; *The Future of Agriculture: IoT, AI and Blockchain Technology for Sustainable Farming,* Betham Science Publisher, 2024
3. Peeyush Kumar et al.; *Affordable Artificial Intelligence: Augmenting Farmer Knowledge with AI,* (FAO/ITU E-Agriculture series, 2021.
4. Tom Duckett et al; *Agricultural Robotics: The Future of Robotic Agriculture,* UK Industrial Strategy White paper Version (Academia), 2018.
5. Andrea Kamilaris & Francesc X. Prenafeta-Boldu; *Deep Learning in Agriculture: A Survey paper, 2018*
6. Pethuru Raj, et al.; *Artificial Intelligence for Precision Agriculure,* CRC Press / Taylor & Francis, 2024.
7. Priyanka Lal & Pradeep Mishra (eds.); *Transforming Agriculture through Artificial Intelligence for Sustainable Food Systems, Academic Press / (via Barnes & Noble), 2024.*
8. Patrick Mukosha; *Career in Information Technology: AI Robotics Engineer, Draft2Digital, 2024, ISBN: 9798224248414*
9. Tofael Ahamed (ed.); *IoT and AI in Agriculture: Self-Sufficiency in Food Production to Achieve Society 5.0 and SDGs Globally, Springer Singapore, 2024.*

Don't miss out!

Visit the website below and you can sign up to receive emails whenever Patrick Mukosha publishes a new book. There's no charge and no obligation.

https://books2read.com/r/B-A-HJNZ-VPPVG

BOOKS 2 READ

Connecting independent readers to independent writers.

Did you love *AI in Agriculture: Farming the Future*? Then you should read *AI Unleashed: The Future of Artificial Intelligence and Human Evolution*[1] by Patrick Mukosha!

[2]

In AI Unleashed: The Future of Artificial Intelligence and Human Evolution, the transformative power of AI is explored as both a force of unparalleled innovation and a challenge to humanity's very essence. This thought-provoking book examines how artificial intelligence is reshaping industries, redefining human potential, and altering the course of evolution itself.From ethical dilemmas and job displacement to breakthroughs in healthcare and creativity, the book unpacks AI's promises and perils. It envisions a future where human intelligence merges with machine capabilities, urging society to embrace this revolution responsibly.A beacon for both optimism

---

1. https://books2read.com/u/4jxX72
2. https://books2read.com/u/4jxX72

and caution, AI Unleashed compels readers to confront how we can harness AI to propel humanity forward while preserving what makes us fundamentally human.

Whether you are an AI enthusiast, a skeptic, or a curious observer of the digital age, this book will leave you inspired, informed, and ready to confront the challenges of the AI-driven future.

Also by Patrick Mukosha

GoodMan

Resilient Strategies: Thriving in Harsh Business Conditions
Strategic Entrepreneurship: Navigating The Path To Success
Decisive Power: Navigating How to Make Toughest Decisions
"Reigning the Boardroom: A Trailblazing Guide to Corporate Governance Success"
Fortifying Digital Fortress: A Comprehensive Guide to Information Systems Security
“Unleashing the Power of Inclusive Innovation: Transforming the World for All”
“Exploring Computer Systems: From Fundamentals to Advanced Concepts”
“Computer Viruses Unveiled: Types, Trends and Mitigation Strategies”
"The Pinnacle of Success: Unveiling the World's 20 Most Successful Brands in 2023”
“Mastering Relational Databases: From Fundamentals to Advanced Concepts”
“Navigating Change: A Comprehensive Guide to Change Management”
“Information Systems Unraveled: Exploring the Core Concepts”
"Careers in Information Technology: Network Engineer"

“Careers in Information Technology: Network and Systems Administrator”
“Careers in Information Technology: Database Administrator”
"Careers in Information Technology: Cybersecurity Analyst"
“Careers in Information Technology: Cloud Security Specialist”
"Careers in Information Technology: Blockchain Developer"
"Careers in Information Technology: DevOps Engineer"
"Careers in Information Technology: Quality Assurance Analyst"
"Careers in Information Technology: Machine Learning Engineer"
"Careers in Information Technology: Artificial Intelligence (AI) Engineer"
"Careers in Information Technology: Internet of Things (IoT) Developer"
"Careers in Information Technology: AR/VR Developer"
“Careers in Information Technology: IoT Embedded Systems Designer”
“Careers in Information Technology: Artificial Intelligence (AI) Robotics Engineer”
“Careers in Information Technology: IoT Solutions Engineer”
“Careers in Information Technology: Data Scientist”
"Careers in Information Technology: Computer Vision Engineer"
"The Sociology of Information Technology"
“Smart Cities: The Technology Transforming Urban Living”
"The Future of Connectivity: Unleashing the Power of 5G and Beyond"
" Cybersecurity 2030 - Strategies for a Secure Digital Future"
The AI-Human Merger: Becoming Super-Intelligent Beings
AI Unleashed: The Future of Artificial Intelligence and Human Evolution
The Digital Prophet: Predicting the Next Decade of Disruption
AI in Agriculture: Farming the Future

About the Author

Patrick Mukosha is an ICT & Management Consultant. With 15+ years of IT experience, he's passionate about all things ICT. He also loves to bring ICT down to a level that everyone can understand. His works have been quoted on Academia by Researchers and ICT Practitioners (www.academia.edu). He has a PHD and MBA from AIU, USA, BSc(Hons) ICT, UEA, UK, Dipl, CCT, UK. He's a founder of PatWest Technologies.

www.ingramcontent.com/pod-product-compliance
Lightning Source LLC
LaVergne TN
LVHW090312210926
848480LV00001B/218

* 9 7 9 8 2 3 0 9 0 6 5 3 7 *